The Complete 2025 LLC Beginner's Guide

5-in-1 Handbook to Starting, Managing, Scaling and Simplified Strategies for Tax Reduction, Building Business Credit, Creating a Winning Marketing Plan, and Maximizing Asset Management.

Peter Harrington

Copyright Notice

© [2024] [Peter Harrington]. All Rights Reserved.

This book is protected by copyright law and may not be reproduced, distributed, or transmitted in any form or by any means, electronic or mechanical, including photocopying, recording, or by any information storage or retrieval system, without the prior written permission of the copyright owner, except for brief quotations used in reviews or scholarly publications.

Disclaimer

The information provided in this book is for educational and informational purposes only. It is not intended as legal, financial, or tax advice and should not be construed as such. While every effort has been made to ensure the accuracy of the content, the author and publisher assume no responsibility for errors or omissions, or for any consequences resulting from the use of the information contained in this book.

Readers are encouraged to seek professional advice before making any financial, legal, or business decisions. The author does not guarantee any specific outcomes or success and disclaims any liability for damages arising from the use of this material.

The content in this book reflects the author's views and is based on information available at the time of writing. Financial laws and regulations may change, and individual circumstances may vary.

TABLE OF CONTENTS

Introduction 15

Chapter 1: Understanding LLC Basics 24

Chapter 2: 2025 LLC Formation- Legal Requirements and Regulations 35

Chapter 3: LLC Taxes—A Breakdown of 2025 Tax Laws 45

Chapter 4: Asset and Liability Protection for LLC Owners 56

Chapter 5: Financial Management for Your LLC 66

Chapter 6: Strategies for Expanding Your LLC 77

Chapter 7: LLC Compliance and Ongoing Maintenance 87

Chapter 8: 2025 LLC Trends and Future-Proofing Your Business 97

Chapter 9: A Comprehensive Guide to LLC Formation 109

Bonus Contents 118

Conclusion 159

QUOTES

"An LLC is not just a legal structure; it's a shield that protects your personal assets while empowering your entrepreneurial spirit." – Anonymous

"Forming an LLC is like building the foundation of a house—it provides structure, protection, and the strength to grow." – Unknown

"In business, liability protection is priceless. An LLC ensures you can focus on your vision without the constant fear of personal financial loss." – Anonymous

"The true value of an LLC lies in its flexibility—it's designed to grow with your business, not restrict it." – Business Consultant

"Your LLC is more than a legal entity; it's a strategy for risk management and business longevity." – Unknown

"With the right LLC setup, you can make the most of tax advantages while safeguarding your personal finances." – Financial Advisor

"The power of an LLC is not in its formation alone, but in the protection and opportunities it provides as your business grows." - Entrepreneur

"An LLC offers the freedom of a partnership with the security of a corporation—it's the best of both worlds." - Business Expert

"In business, risks are inevitable. But with an LLC, you can ensure that those risks don't have to fall on your personal assets." - Legal Advisor

"Building a successful business starts with making the right legal decisions, and choosing an LLC is one of the smartest moves you can make for both protection and flexibility." - Business Consultant

TESTIMONIALS

Emma J. - Entrepreneur & Owner of Fresh Blooms Florist

"This guide was exactly what I needed! As a first-time business owner, I was overwhelmed by the idea of forming an LLC and navigating all the legal and tax requirements. The step-by-step instructions made it easy to understand, and the real-world examples helped me put everything into practice. I feel confident and well-prepared for the next phase of growth. The bonuses, especially the business resource toolkit, were invaluable. Highly recommend!"

Mark T. - Freelance Consultant and LLC Owner

"I've been running my consulting business for a couple of years now, but this book opened my eyes to so many things I was overlooking. From taxes to liability protection, it gave me the clarity I needed to optimize my LLC. I especially appreciated the sections on managing finances and business credit cards — those are game changers! The guide is straightforward, practical, and easy to follow. I wish I'd had this when I first started!"

Sofia R. - Owner of Peak Performance Coaching

"The 2025 LLC Beginner's Guide is a must-read for any small business owner. It covers everything from legal requirements to marketing strategies, and I now feel equipped to manage my LLC more effectively. I especially loved the chapters on liability protection and building business credit. The bonuses are a huge added benefit – tools I can use right away to streamline my operations. Thank you for creating such a comprehensive resource!"

James K. - Co-Founder of UrbanTech Solutions

"We've been operating our LLC for over a year, but this guide has been a game-changer for us. It helped us understand the nuances of LLC management and provided actionable insights on how to scale our business. The chapter on tax laws was especially timely with all the recent changes in 2025. I feel more confident about our growth strategy and how we can avoid potential pitfalls in the future. Worth every penny!"

Rachel D. - Online Retailer & LLC Owner

"Starting an LLC for my online retail business seemed intimidating at first, but this book made the whole process much easier to navigate. The guide's practical advice, combined with up-to-date information on new regulations and tax laws for 2025, was exactly what I needed. The bonus content on business insurance and marketing strategy is incredibly valuable, and I've already started applying some of the tips. This book is a great investment for any entrepreneur looking to set up or manage an LLC!"

A Heartfelt Thank You

Thank you for choosing the 2025 LLC Beginner's Guide. Whether you're a first-time entrepreneur or an experienced business owner, taking the time to invest in your knowledge and your business is a significant step toward success. Your decision to dive into this guide reflects your dedication to building a strong foundation for your LLC—one that will support you through the challenges, triumphs, and growth in the years to come.

This book was created with the intention of helping you navigate the complex world of LLCs, simplify the process, and provide you with the tools and insights you need to make informed, confident decisions. It is my hope that you not only find value in the practical steps and expert advice but that you feel empowered to take your business to new heights.

Starting and managing an LLC is no small feat. But with the right knowledge, support, and strategies, you can build a successful, sustainable business. I am truly grateful to be a part of your journey, and I look forward to seeing how this guide helps you create the future you envision for your LLC.

Thank you for trusting me with your entrepreneurial journey.

With sincere gratitude,

ABOUT THE AUTHOR

I've always believed that entrepreneurship is a journey that requires more than just passion and hard work; it requires the right strategies, structures, and guidance. I've been fortunate enough to experience the highs and lows of starting and growing businesses across different industries. Over the years, I've founded three companies, each starting small and gradually scaling up. While each venture had its own unique challenges, the common thread was the need for a solid foundation, which started with choosing the right legal structure—specifically, the LLC.

Looking back at my first business, I remember feeling both excited and overwhelmed. I knew that in order to succeed, I needed to protect my personal assets while having the flexibility to adapt and grow. That's when I first stumbled upon the idea of forming an LLC. At the time, I didn't fully grasp the power of this business structure. But as my business expanded, I realized how crucial the right legal and financial structure was for managing risks, optimizing taxes, and ensuring sustainability.

Through trial and error, I learned what worked and what didn't. I encountered challenges when trying to navigate taxes, compliance, and liability issues. But with each lesson, I refined my approach, adjusting strategies to better protect my companies and their future. By the time I launched my third business, I had a much clearer understanding of the nuances of LLCs, and how they could be leveraged to secure long-term growth and profitability.

It was this experience—building multiple companies from the ground up—that inspired me to write this book. I know what it's like to be an entrepreneur at the start of a journey, feeling like you're in over your head. The legal side of running a business can be intimidating, and that's why I'm passionate about helping others avoid the mistakes I made. I want to help you set up your LLC right from the start, navigate the complexities of business taxes, protect your assets, and ensure your business is positioned for success.

The reason I'm the right person to write this book is because I've lived through the exact challenges this guide addresses. I've been in your shoes — wondering how to make sense of business regulations, how to separate personal and business finances, and how to scale while staying compliant. But more importantly, I've also discovered the strategies that made all

the difference. I've gone through the struggle of building a business from a small idea to a thriving company, and along the way, I learned that the right legal structure and financial management are at the heart of any successful venture.

Now, having scaled my businesses and learned firsthand what works and what doesn't, I feel compelled to share that knowledge. This book is more than just a manual on how to form an LLC. It's a reflection of my own journey and the lessons I've learned along the way. If I can help even one entrepreneur avoid the mistakes I made or make the process smoother for someone just starting out, then writing this book will have been worth it.

In the end, this guide is not just for people looking to form an LLC; it's for anyone who wants to set their business up for long-term success. Whether you're thinking about starting an LLC or you already have one, the strategies in this book are the same ones I've used to safeguard my companies, optimize my taxes, and scale my business. With the knowledge I'm sharing here, I hope you feel empowered to take your LLC to the next level, just as I have done with my own businesses.

Writing this book is my way of giving back. It's my way of helping entrepreneurs like you avoid the pitfalls I encountered and make informed decisions that will positively impact the future of your business. It's my story, but it's also your roadmap to a successful LLC.

INTRODUCTION

Starting a business is an entrepreneur's most exciting and challenging decision. As the business landscape changes, selecting the best structure for your firm is an important decision that affects everything from taxes to legal responsibilities. Among the different options available, the Limited Liability Company (LLC) has emerged as a top choice for businesses in recent years, and it is expected to remain so in 2025. This guide will help you manage the intricacies of founding, operating, and maximizing an LLC, ensuring you make the right decisions for your organization.

WHY CHOOSE AN LLC IN 2025

Due to its flexibility, an LLC is frequently the favored business structure for entrepreneurs, freelancers, and small business owners. In 2025, the picture for LLCs remains favorable, albeit with some critical caveats. Let's go over why an LLC can be the best option for your business:

1. Liability Protection.

The major reason many businesses join an LLC is to safeguard themselves against personal responsibility. As a business owner, your personal assets, such as your home and money, are in danger if your company is sued or goes bankrupt. However, LLCs protect their owners (members) from personal liability for corporate debts or lawsuits. If the LLC is sued or goes bankrupt, your personal property and funds are usually secured, giving you peace of mind while running your business.

2. Flexible Tax Treatment

One of the primary benefits of establishing an LLC is the tax freedom it provides. LLCs are automatically classified as pass-through entities for tax purposes, meaning the business does not pay taxes directly. Instead, revenues and losses are "passed through" to the owners, who record them on their individual tax returns. This prevents double taxation for corporations. However, LLCs can be taxed as S or C Corporations, providing extra tax benefits based on your business structure and objectives. This flexibility allows you to select the tax treatment that best meets your needs and may result in significant savings.

3. Operational flexibility.

LLCs allow business owners to establish their firms appropriately for their individual needs. Whether you are the lone member of your LLC or have several partners, the operating agreement can be adapted to your needs. Unlike corporations, LLCs require fewer formalities to manage. An LLC is not required to have annual meetings or elect a board of directors, making it easier to administer for entrepreneurs who prefer a more flexible form.

4. Credibility among clients and partners.

Operating as an LLC can help your firm gain credibility, making it appear more established and professional to clients, suppliers, and partners. While you might operate as a sole proprietorship or partnership, an LLC shows you are serious about your company and its long-term success. This can make attracting customers, obtaining finance, and establishing commercial ties easier.

5. Growth Potential

Another important reason to choose an LLC is the flexibility to scale. As your firm grows, an LLC allows you to recruit partners, generate financing, and extend your operations. Whether you wish to add more members or attract investors, the LLC form can support a variety of growth scenarios. This makes it an excellent choice for entrepreneurs who intend to expand their business over time.

Despite these advantages, incorporating an LLC is not without challenges. State-specific regulations, registration costs, and maintenance need to be aware of. Learning how to organize, administer, and maximize your LLC is essential, especially in 2025 when legal and tax laws are continually changing.

WHAT YOU WILL LEARN FROM THIS GUIDE

This tutorial will help you through founding an LLC, explaining its benefits, and managing its operations successfully. This is what you will find inside:

Breakdown

1. Understanding LLC Basics and Benefits

We'll start with a simple explanation of what an LLC is, how it works, and why it's a popular choice for entrepreneurs. This chapter will discuss its main advantages: liability protection, tax flexibility, and operational ease.

2. Steps to Form an LLC in 2025.

This chapter details the steps involved in incorporating an LLC, from selecting a name to filing the proper paperwork with your state. We'll walk you through the process and give you ideas on how to prevent frequent blunders.

3. Understanding the 2025 LLC regulations and tax laws.

Staying current on the newest legal changes affecting LLCs is critical. This chapter will review the 2025 regulations, including state-specific restrictions, new tax laws, and any recent changes to LLC tax classification that may affect your business.

4. Managing Your LLC and Maintaining Compliance

Running an LLC entails more than simply registering it. We'll go over how to efficiently run your LLC, from financial management to state and federal legislation compliance. This chapter also examines the significance of operating agreements, annual reporting, and record keeping.

5. Tax strategies and deductions for LLC owners.

We'll discuss the tax benefits of owning an LLC and ideas for increasing your deductions. Whether you're paying taxes as a single-member LLC or choosing S-corp status, this chapter will give you practical advice on how to lower your tax bill.

6. Managing business finances and establishing credit

Managing finances is an important aspect of business success. This chapter explains how to open business accounts, manage cash flow, and establish business credit. We'll also review how to successfully utilize business credit cards to segregate your personal and corporate finances, establish credit, and maximize rewards.

7. Scaling your LLC for growth.

If you want to grow your business, we'll examine how an LLC structure can help. This includes increasing membership, soliciting investment, and growing operations. We'll also discuss how to alter your LLC as your firm grows.

HOW TO USE THIS GUIDE TO MAXIMIZE YOUR LLC'S POTENTIAL

This guide is more than simply a reference manual; it is a comprehensive resource that will help you make informed decisions regarding your LLC throughout its life cycle. Here's how to apply it effectively:

1. Step-by-Step Approach.

Each chapter builds on the previous one, so reading them in order is better. As you work through the guide, you'll better grasp the complexities of LLC creation, management, and tax tactics.

2. Practical Action Steps

Each chapter ends with specific tasks and checklists to help you get through the process. Take your time with these methods and apply them to your business circumstances. For example, when forming an LLC, the checklist will assist you in ensuring that every item is addressed, from state registration to creating an operating agreement.

3. Refer back as needed.

This guide is intended to be a resource you can refer to as needed. If you need help comprehending new tax rules or are considering expanding your firm, check and return to the relevant chapters for advice.

4. Maximize your bonuses.

This guide includes essential supplemental content such as templates, worksheets, and additional resources. Download and utilize these tools to help you make better decisions and enhance your company processes.

By the end of this tutorial, you will have the knowledge and tools you need to start, operate, and optimize your LLC in 2025 and beyond. Whether you're just starting out or seeking to expand, this resource can help you make sound decisions to position your company for long-term success.

CHAPTER 1: UNDERSTANDING LLC BASICS

Starting a business requires several key decisions, one of which is determining the best business structure. Limited Liability Companies (LLCs) have grown in popularity in recent years because they provide various benefits to business owners. This chapter will explain what an LLC is, how it differs from other business forms, and why it can be a good fit for your endeavor. We'll also examine the many LLC forms, their primary benefits, and step-by-step instructions on starting one.

WHAT IS AN LLC

A Limited Liability Company (LLC) is a legal structure that combines a corporation's and a partnership's advantages. It is intended to shield the owners from personal liability while providing the flexibility of a partnership in terms of management and taxes. An LLC offers the legal protections of

a corporation while allowing business owners (known as "members") to govern their organization with less formality than corporations do.

The most significant feature of an LLC is that it keeps personal assets distinct from company responsibilities. If your LLC is sued or incurs debt, your personal assets (such as your home, car, or money) are normally safeguarded. This structure appeals to small business owners, entrepreneurs, and freelancers who wish to reduce personal risk while keeping operational flexibility.

HOW LLCS DIFFER FROM OTHER BUSINESS STRUCTURES

When launching a business, it's critical to understand how an LLC compares to other typical business structures like sole proprietorships, partnerships, and corporations. Here's the breakdown:

- The sole proprietorship is the simplest business structure. A sole proprietorship is not a separate legal entity from the owner; hence, the business and the owner are considered the same. The main disadvantage is that the owner is personally liable for debts and liabilities, which means personal assets may be at stake.

- Partnerships, like sole proprietorships, enable two or more persons to run a business jointly. However, each partner is liable for the business's debts and liabilities. A general partnership, in particular, holds all partners personally liable for the business's conduct. Although limited partnerships (LP) and limited liability partnerships (LLP) provide some protections, these arrangements often involve greater risk than an LLC.

- A corporation is a formal structure that functions independently from its shareholders. While companies provide the most comprehensive personal responsibility protection, they are subject to additional rules and tougher restrictions, such as a board of directors, annual meetings, and more complex tax structures. Furthermore, corporations incur "double taxation," which means the company is taxed on profits while shareholders are taxed on any dividends received.

In contrast, an LLC provides greater flexibility with fewer formalities than a corporation and liability protection without the same amount of complexity. It combines the finest features of partnerships and corporations, making it an excellent option for many entrepreneurs.

KEY ADVANTAGES OF FORMING AN LLC

One of the primary reasons business owners chose the LLC structure is because it provides liability protection, tax flexibility, and operational convenience. Let's look at each of these advantages in greater detail:

1. Limited Liability Protection.

The most major benefit of incorporating an LLC is likely limited liability protection. This means that the that the owners (members) are not personally liable for the company's debts and legal obligations. If your LLC is sued or the company goes bankrupt, your personal assets — such as your home, car, or personal savings — are typically safeguarded. This protection is critical for business owners who want to minimize the danger of losing personal assets in the case of a lawsuit or financial difficulties.

However, there are several exceptions to the norm. If you personally guarantee a business loan, engage in unlawful activities, or fail to follow LLC procedures (such as keeping separate financial records for the business), you may lose your limited liability protection. Your LLC must be a unique legal entity to maintain this protection.

2. Pass-through Taxation

One of the most appealing aspects of an LLC is the pass-through tax benefit. Unlike corporations, which are taxed on earnings and then have shareholders pay taxes on dividends (leading to double taxation), LLCs do not typically pay federal income taxes at the business level. Instead, the company's revenues and losses are "passed through" to the owners' individual tax returns.

Each member reports their portion of the LLC's profits and losses on their tax return, resulting in a more straightforward and potentially lower tax liability. For example, if the LLC makes $100,000 in profit, each member pays taxes on their portion, not the entire amount.

This tax structure is frequently more advantageous for small business owners and entrepreneurs because it eliminates the complex and costly double taxation that corporations incur. LLC owners can also deduct company expenses directly, which reduces their taxable income.

3. Operational flexibility.

LLCs provide greater operational flexibility than other

business arrangements. Corporations are not required to observe any precise rules regarding board meetings, shareholder voting, or other formalities. An LLC can be governed by its members (owners) or designated managers, allowing business owners to customize the management structure to their needs.

Furthermore, LLCs are exempt from the standard corporate obligations of issuing shares, holding annual meetings, and keeping minutes. This adaptability makes LLCs simpler and less expensive to run. Members can direct how the firm is operated, how earnings are distributed, and how decisions are made, providing a high level of control.

LLCs can also have infinite members without restrictions on who can join. This makes LLCs a viable alternative for enterprises of all kinds, from sole proprietorships to huge partnerships.

TYPES OF LLCS (SINGLE MEMBER VS. MULTI-MEMBER)

LLCs are divided into two categories based on the number of members (owners):

- Single-member LLCs are owned by a single individual. This is a popular option for freelancers, consultants, and small business owners who desire the liability protection and tax advantages of an LLC without collaborating with others. Single-member LLCs are disregarded entities for tax purposes, which means the IRS treats them as a sole proprietorship. The owner includes the LLC's revenue and costs on their personal tax return.

- A multi-member LLC comprises two or more owners who share the business's revenues and losses. Multi-member LLCs are taxed as partnerships, and the money is distributed to the owners, who record their respective gains or losses on their personal tax returns. The operating agreement for a multi-member LLC normally specifies how profits are distributed and what responsibilities each member has.

While both LLC types provide limited liability protection, the main distinction is the management structure and number of members. Single- and multi-member LLCs offer the same liability protection and tax benefits.

THE STEPS TO FORM AN LLC

Forming an LLC is a simple process but requires close attention to detail. Here's a summary of the actions you'll need to take:

1. Choose a Business Name: The first step in forming an LLC is to select a distinctive name that follows your state's LLC naming laws. The name must be distinct from other registered business names in your state and include the term "LLC" or "Limited Liability Company."

2. Choose a Registered Agent: This individual or business organization will receive legal documents for your LLC. This might be you or a third-party service, but the registered agent must have a physical address in the state where your LLC is established.

3. File Articles of Organization: This formal document establishes your LLC. It contains fundamental information about your company, such as its name, address, registration agent, and whether it will be run by members or management. Articles of Organization must be submitted with the Secretary of State or a similar entity in your state.

4. Create an Operating Agreement: Although not needed in all states, it is strongly advised for all LLCs. This document details how your LLC will be administered, how earnings and losses will be allocated, and what happens if one of the members leaves. It helps to avert disagreements and keeps the business running smoothly.

5. Obtain an Employer Identification Number (EIN): Most LLCs need an EIN from the IRS. This number is similar to a Social Security number for your business and is required for tax purposes, recruiting staff, and opening business bank accounts.

6. Register for state taxes: Depending on your state and the nature of your business, you may be required to register for state-level taxes, such as sales or employment tax. Check with your state's tax department to see what's needed.

7. Comply with State and Local Requirements: Some states and municipalities may demand additional business licenses or permits. Make sure you verify with the local authorities to guarantee compliance.

These procedures allow you to legally incorporate and operate an LLC, laying the groundwork for your company's success.

CHAPTER 2: 2025 LLC FORMATION- LEGAL REQUIREMENTS AND REGULATIONS

Forming a Limited Liability Company (LLC) entails more than selecting a name and opening a company bank account. The procedure involves navigating legal and regulatory regulations, which can differ based on the state where you incorporate the LLC. This chapter reviews the crucial procedures to effectively form your LLC, from selecting the correct state to understanding the required documentation. We'll also review the important legislative developments in 2025 so you're fully aware and ready to start your business.

HOW TO SELECT THE RIGHT STATE FOR YOUR LLC

The first step in forming an LLC is deciding which state to register your firm. Although you may believe incorporating an LLC in your home state is the most straightforward option, this is not necessarily true. Each state has its own set of rules, fees, and tax requirements, which can have a big impact on your firm.

1. Home vs. Other States

Many entrepreneurs assume that they must register an LLC in the state where they intend to operate. While this is usually the simplest option, there are several situations where incorporating an LLC in another state may be helpful. States such as Delaware, Nevada, and Wyoming are known for their business-friendly legislation that provides tax breaks, asset protection, and minimum reporting requirements.

2. Factors to Consider while Choosing a State.

- **State Taxes: Some states** (e.g., Florida, Texas, and Wyoming) have no income tax, which can be appealing to business owners. Others may charge franchise taxes or other business-related expenses.

- **Formation Fees:** The cost of founding and sustaining an LLC varies by state. Delaware, for example, levies a franchise tax dependent on the type of business, whereas California has substantial yearly taxes for limited liability companies.

- **Delaware and Nevada** are popular states for their privacy and asset protection laws, which allow owners to remain anonymous.

- **Ease of administration:** Certain states make organizing and maintaining an LLC easier. Wyoming and Delaware are noted for their efficient processes and low red tape.

Incorporating an LLC may be the easiest and most cost-effective solution if your company only operates in one state. However, if you intend to expand throughout multiple states or have unique asset protection concerns, it may be worthwhile to consider other states.

IMPORTANT LEGAL FORMS AND DOCUMENTS YOU NEED

Once you've decided on a state, the following step is to create the legal documents required to properly incorporate an LLC. These documents verify that your LLC is correctly created, consistent with state laws, and ready to conduct business. The most essential legal papers are:

Articles of Organization

This is the foundational document required to create your LLC. The Articles of Organization, also called a Certificate of Formation in some states, are filed with the Secretary of State's office. The document includes basic information about your LLC, such as:

- The name of the LLC
- The address of the business
- The registered agent's name and address
- The duration of the LLC (usually perpetual, unless specified otherwise)

Operating Agreement

While not always legally required, an **Operating Agreement** is crucial for defining the ownership structure and operating procedures of your LLC. This internal document outlines how the LLC will be run, including:

- The percentage of ownership for each member
- Member duties and responsibilities
- Profit and loss distribution
- Decision-making processes and dispute resolution

- Member exit and succession planning

Having an Operating Agreement in place helps prevent future misunderstandings and provides clarity in case of legal disputes.

LLC NAME REQUIREMENTS AND TRADEMARK CONSIDERATIONS

Choosing the correct name for your LLC is an important step that requires legal and branding considerations. Your LLC's name will be the first image your clients or customers get of your company, and it must also adhere to state rules. Here's something to remember:

1. State Naming Rules.

Each state has its own set of restrictions about which terms can and cannot be used in the name of an LLC. Generally, the name must include the words "Limited Liability Company" or an abbreviation like "LLC" or "L.L.C." It cannot involve terminology that could confuse your LLC and a government agency (for example, FBI, Treasury Department).

2. Name Availability.

Before you choose a name, be sure it isn't already in use. Most states have internet databases where you may look up existing LLC names to ensure yours is unique. If your name has already been taken, you must choose a different one.

3. Trademark considerations.

In addition to verifying state databases, federal trademark registration is necessary if you want your LLC name to be protected nationwide. A trademark assures that no other company in your field may use the same or a confusingly similar name. The United States Patent and Trademark Office (USPTO) provides an online search engine to help you discover whether your name qualifies for trademark protection.

FILING THE ARTICLES OF ORGANIZATION AND OPERATING AGREEMENT.

The Articles of Organization are filed with your state's Secretary of State, legally establishing your LLC. This is an important step since it marks the official formation of your LLC in the eyes of the state.

Once the Articles are filed, you may be issued a Certificate of Formation or Articles of Organization, which documents that your LLC exists. After acquiring this document, you can open a business bank account, apply for necessary permits, and start operations.

While the Operating Agreement is not required in all states, it is strongly advised that you explain the internal operations of your LLC. To avoid future disagreements, have this contract created and agreed to by all members before formally incorporating your LLC. Without an Operating Agreement, the LLC's operations will be governed by state laws, which may not be for the members' precise purposes.

UNDERSTANDING REGISTERED AGENTS AND THEIR ROLES

A Registered Agent is an individual or business entity authorized to receive legal documents on behalf of the LLC. This includes government notices, tax forms, and legal documents such as lawsuits. The Registered Agent plays an important function because the LLC must legally have one.

1. Who Can Become a Registered Agent

The Registered Agent's physical address must be where the LLC is registered. This can be a third-party service (many firms use professional Registered Agent services) or an individual who fits the qualifications, such as a business owner or employee. Some states allow you to operate as your Registered Agent, but you should consider privacy and dependability before going down this path.

2. Why Do You Need a Registered Agent

The Registered Agent guarantees that your LLC complies with state rules by receiving and processing crucial legal and tax paperwork. This safeguards your company against missing deadlines or legal notices, which could result in penalties or default judgments.

NEW LLC REGULATIONS FOR 2025: KEY CHANGES YOU SHOULD KNOW

The year 2025 introduced many modifications to LLC legislation that every business owner should know. These modifications simplify the LLC formation process, improve transparency, and answer emergent company needs in a quickly evolving legal landscape. Key changes to keep in mind are:

1. Changes in state-specific fees and taxes.

Some states, including California, New York, and Texas, have revised LLC creation fees and annual maintenance rates. California, for example, has increased its annual franchise tax for limited liability companies, while Texas has implemented additional reporting requirements for enterprises outside of the state.

2. New compliance rules for multi-state LLCs.

The 2025 laws have tightened the limits for LLCs who do business in numerous states. Businesses are now required to complete additional documentation and maybe pay fees in every state where they operate, regardless of where their LLC is registered.

3. Increased Privacy and Security Regulations.

Due to growing privacy concerns, numerous states have passed legislation mandating LLCs to reveal beneficial ownership or the individuals who ultimately run the corporation. These rules are intended to increase transparency and prevent money laundering or fraud.

4. Tax Law Updates for LLCs

The IRS has changed its regulations for LLCs seeking S-Corporation registration, emphasizing the classification of owners and how self-employment taxes are handled. LLCs must now file additional documents to be eligible for the new tax breaks announced in 2025.

Understanding and applying these legal developments to your LLC formation procedure can help you keep your business compliant and avoid costly penalties.

CHAPTER 3: LLC TAXES—A BREAKDOWN OF 2025 TAX LAWS.

Understanding taxes is one of the most crucial components of operating an LLC. While incorporating an LLC offers some legal benefits, it does not automatically reduce your tax responsibilities. Although an LLC's tax structure is flexible, it also brings additional complexity that business owners must understand. This chapter will review the important components of LLC taxation in 2025, such as how taxes vary depending on how your LLC is taxed, self-employment taxes, new deductions, and the impact of recent tax law changes.

BASICS OF LLC TAXATION: SOLE PROPRIETORSHIP VS. S-CORP VS. C-CORPORATION

One of the primary advantages of having an LLC is the flexibility in how it can be taxed. An LLC is automatically classified as a pass-through entity for tax purposes, meaning the business does not pay taxes. Instead, gains and losses are "passed through" to the members' individual tax returns. However, LLC owners can choose between many tax classes, each with benefits and drawbacks. The three most frequent tax choices for LLCs are:

1. Sole Proprietorship (Default Taxation of Single-Member LLCs)

The IRS treats a single-member LLC as a sole proprietorship by default. This indicates that the LLC is not taxed individually. Instead, the owner uses Schedule C to include the business's income and costs on their personal tax return. The business's profits are subject to self-employment taxes, including Social Security and Medicare. This structure is straightforward. However, it does not provide the same tax benefits as other structures.

2. S-Corp Election

LLC owners can elect to have their business taxed as an S-Corporation by completing Form 2553 with the IRS. This option can result in considerable tax savings, particularly for LLC owners who earn a substantial salary from the business. Unlike a sole proprietorship or partnership, S-Corp taxation permits owners to deduct a portion of the LLC's revenues as dividends rather than wages. These dividends are not subject to self-employment tax, which can result in significant savings.

To qualify as an S-Corp, an LLC must meet specific criteria, such as having fewer than 100 shareholders (members), being a domestic corporation, and having just one class of stock.

3. C-Corporation Election

An LLC can also be taxed as a C-Corporation by completing Form 8832. This option is less popular for smaller enterprises, but it may be advantageous for LLCs that intend to reinvest profits back into the company or anticipate significant development. C-Corporations are subject to corporate income tax rates, which may be more favorable for certain enterprises. However, profits are taxed at the corporate level and, when dispersed to shareholders as dividends, resulting in double taxation.

Choosing between these solutions necessitates careful analysis of your business objectives, estimated income, and growth strategy. Consulting with a tax specialist can assist you in making the most tax-efficient decision for your particular scenario.

SELF-EMPLOYMENT TAXES: WHAT YOU SHOULD KNOW

Self-employment taxes are a major worry for LLC owners, particularly those taxed as sole proprietorships or partnerships. In 2025, the self-employment tax rate will continue at 15.3%, divided into two parts:

- Up to a particular income threshold, Social Security pays 12.4%.

- Medicare pays 2.9%, with an additional 0.9% for high incomes (above $200,000 for single filers or $250,000 for married couples filing jointly).

This tax is based on your net profits from self-employment and must be reported using Schedule SE. If your LLC is taxed as a sole proprietorship or partnership, the tax applies to all of your profits, which is why many LLC owners choose the S-Corp form to decrease their self-employment tax burden by paying out a portion of their business revenue as dividends.

NEW TAX DEDUCTIONS FOR LLCS IN 2025.

Tax breaks are one of the primary benefits of establishing an LLC. Several tax changes are set to take effect in 2025, which may benefit LLC owners by allowing them to deduct more company expenses. These deductions can reduce your LLC's taxable revenue, lowering your tax liability.

1. Business Expense Deductions

LLC owners can deduct a wide variety of business expenses, including:

- Office supplies
- Marketing and advertising costs
- Travel expenses related to business

- Utilities and rent

- Professional services fees (e.g., attorney, accountant)

The IRS allows LLC owners to deduct any **ordinary and necessary** expenses that are required for running the business. In 2025, the IRS has streamlined some of the criteria for deductible expenses, making it easier to claim deductions for business-related equipment and supplies.

2. Home Office Tax Deduction

The **home office deduction** has been a valuable tax break for small business owners working from home. In 2025, the IRS continues to allow LLC owners who use part of their home exclusively for business purposes to deduct expenses related to that space, including:

- Rent or mortgage interest

- Utilities

- Insurance

- Depreciation of the home

The IRS provides two methods for calculating the home office deduction: the **simplified method** (which allows a deduction of $5 per square foot up to 300 square feet) and the **regular method**, which requires you to calculate actual expenses based on the percentage of your home used for business.

3. Vehicle Expense Deductions.

If you drive your vehicle for business purposes, you can deduct either your actual expenses (fuel, repairs, insurance, etc.) or the IRS-set standard mileage rate each year. For 2025, the normal mileage rate has been modified for inflation, making it easier for many LLC owners to compute and claim. Keep accurate records of business miles driven to support your deductions.

RECENT TAX LAW CHANGES: HOW THEY AFFECT LLCS IN 2025

The tax laws governing LLCs vary every year. Several important updates for 2025 may affect how LLCs file taxes and claim deductions:

1. Changes in Pass-Through Taxation

While pass-through taxation remains the default for LLCs, several changes were made in 2025 to clarify how specific business revenue is taxed. Notably, the IRS has modified the Qualified Business Income (QBI) deductions requirements. LLC owners whose business income is designated as QBI may have more chances to decrease taxable income, particularly if the LLC operates in specific industries or fits IRS-set standards.

2. Updated Deduction Limits and Rules

The 2025 tax laws also include changes to the limits on some types of deductions. For example, the Section 179 Deduction (which lets businesses write off the cost of eligible property in the year it is purchased) has been increased. This means that LLCs can write off larger amounts for business equipment and property, resulting in an immediate tax benefit rather than depreciating such assets over time.

HIRING EMPLOYEES VERSUS CONTRACTORS: TAX IMPLICATIONS

When hiring for your LLC, it is critical to understand the tax ramifications of hiring employees rather than independent contractors. Employees are liable to payroll taxes, and as an employer, you must match their Social Security and Medicare contributions. In contrast, independent contractors are responsible for paying their own self-employment taxes, which can save your LLC money on payroll taxes.

However, misclassifying employees as contractors can result in penalties, so it is vital to grasp the IRS's standards and make the correct decision.

HOW TO FILE YOUR LLC TAXES (FORMS 1065, SCHEDULE C, AND MORE)

Filing taxes for your LLC is determined by its tax classification. If your LLC is taxed as a sole proprietorship or partnership, you will file Form 1065, which details the LLC's revenue, deductions, gains, and losses. Additionally, each member of a multi-member LLC must file Schedule K-1 to

record their part of the LLC's income and expenses on their tax return.

For S-Corp tax purposes, the LLC must file Form 1120S and distribute Schedule K-1 to each member. Single-member LLCs taxed as sole proprietorships will report revenue and expenses on Schedule C, connected to your personal tax return (Form 1040).

To avoid difficulties with the IRS, keep accurate records of all business-related revenue and spending and any supporting paperwork.

Navigating LLC taxes can be difficult, especially with the modifications implemented in 2025. Understanding these tax laws and working with a skilled tax professional will help your LLC comply with IRS regulations and maximize possible deductions. This will allow you to concentrate on expanding your business while lowering your tax burden.

CHAPTER 4: ASSET AND LIABILITY PROTECTION FOR LLC OWNERS

The degree of personal asset protection offered by an LLC is one of the primary factors influencing entrepreneurs' decisions to create one. In the event of a lawsuit or corporate debt, your personal assets, including your home, vehicle, and savings, may be in danger if the proper legal structure isn't in place. Although establishing an LLC aid in protecting these assets, doing so calls for additional steps. This chapter will cover the following topics: the function of insurance, the significance of an operating agreement, how LLCs provide liability protection, and how to steer clear of typical mistakes that could compromise your security. We'll also review ways to shield your company from litigation and other legal issues.

HOW LLCS SAFEGUARD YOUR INDIVIDUAL PROPERTY

Establishing an LLC makes the company a different legal entity from its owners or members. This implies that the LLC can sign contracts, accrue debt, and be sued under its name. The limited liability an LLC offers its members is its greatest benefit. In essence, an LLC's members are not held personally liable for the debts or obligations of the company.

For instance, only the LLC's assets — not your personal belongings — are in danger if your LLC is sued or accrues debt. This is a significant difference from partnerships or sole proprietorships, where owners are individually responsible for the company's debts. One of the main factors influencing the LLC structure's popularity among business owners is its legal protection.

Limited liability is not absolute, though. Below, we'll explore the circumstances and behaviors that can lead to protection failure.

LLCS' REQUIREMENTS FOR BUSINESS INSURANCE

Even though an LLC provides liability protection, it's important to realize that this protection isn't always 100% reliable. Personal assets may still be at risk in some situations, especially regarding company insurance. Insurance is essential for protecting the company and its owners.

1. General Liability Insurance: This is the most fundamental type of business insurance. It guards against typical dangers, including property damage, slip-and-fall incidents, and other third-party lawsuits. This coverage guarantees that you won't be held personally responsible for mishaps on your company's property or as a result of your operations.

2. Professional Liability Insurance: Also known as errors and omissions insurance, professional liability insurance is crucial for companies that provide services like consulting or guidance. It guards against allegations that your clients suffered financial losses due to your advice or services.

3. Workers' Compensation Insurance: The government frequently mandates workers' compensation insurance if you have employees. It pays for lost income and medical costs for workers hurt on the job.

4. Property Insurance: This type of coverage guards the tangible assets of your company, such as buildings, machinery, and stock. Coverage guarantees your financial security in the event of damage, theft, or natural disasters, regardless of whether you own or rent your property.

Although an LLC offers legal liability protection, you can strengthen that protection and preserve your personal and corporate assets by obtaining sufficient insurance coverage.

THE SIGNIFICANCE OF AN OPERATING AGREEMENT

The operating agreement is one of the most important papers for an LLC. The LLC's ownership structure, duties, and operating processes are described in this document. An operating agreement is highly advised for several reasons, even if some jurisdictions do not require it.

1. Clearly Defines Ownership and Management: The operating agreement lays out the rights and obligations of each member as well as the management of the LLC. It outlines the ownership stake held by each member and the decision-making process for multi-member LLCs.

2. Prevents disagreements: The operating agreement helps LLC members avoid disagreements by addressing possible conflicts up front. It describes how to handle disputes, add or remove members, and, if required, dissolve the LLC.

3. Legal Protection: The LLC will be subject to the state's default regulations without an operating agreement. It's possible that these default guidelines don't reflect the owners' intentions. In addition to ensuring that the LLC is operated according to the members' desires, a customized operating agreement offers extra protection if the LLC is challenged in court.

4. Strengthens Liability Protection: The operating agreement further strengthens the distinct relationship between the LLC and its members. A court may view the LLC and its owners as a single entity if it lacks an operating agreement, which raises the possibility of personal liability in case of legal problems.

To put it briefly, an operating agreement is a fundamental contract that guarantees the smooth operation of your LLC, reduces disputes and offers a degree of defense against future legal issues.

HOW TO KEEP THE CORPORATE VEIL FROM BEING PIERCED

The protection of personal assets is among an LLC's most important advantages. This protection is not unqualified, though. A court may decide that the LLC is merely an extension of its members if it is not properly managed; this is referred to as penetrating the corporate veil. As a result, members would be held personally liable for the company's debts and liabilities.

It is crucial to follow a few essential procedures in order to prevent this scenario:

1. Keep Separate Finances: The LLC and its members must be considered distinct legal entities. This entails establishing a business bank account and maintaining financial separation between personal and business affairs. Combining the two may give the impression that the LLC is not a distinct legal entity.

2. Adhere to Legal Formalities: LLCs must adhere to certain legal formalities even though they are less formal than corporations. This entails scheduling frequent meetings, keeping accurate records, and submitting yearly reports to the state.

3. Sufficient Capitalization: The LLC needs sufficient money to pay its liabilities and operating costs. Members may be personally liable if an LLC lacks the necessary funds to fulfil its responsibilities.

4. Clear of fraudulent activity: Piercing the corporate veil can occur from any attempt to commit crimes, utilize the LLC for personal benefit, or mislead creditors. Operating the LLC honestly and openly is crucial.

Your LLC's liability protection can be preserved by keeping accurate documents, keeping monies segregated, and abiding by the law.

DEFENDING YOUR COMPANY AGAINST CLAIMS AND LAWSUITS

While creating an LLC and getting the proper insurance will assist in shielding your personal assets, lawsuits and claims can still affect your company. The following tactics can help protect your LLC from future legal issues:

1. Limit Personal Guarantees: Many businesses owners risk losing their personal assets if their company fails by signing personal guarantees for loans or leases. If feasible, refrain from signing personal guarantees and get legal advice to consider your choices.

2. Make Use of Contracts: Having carefully crafted agreements with clients, suppliers, and staff can shield your company from lawsuits alleging carelessness, contract violations, and other legal issues. Contracts should always detail terms, obligations, and dispute resolution processes.

3. Maintain Thorough Records: In the event of a lawsuit, thorough records of financial transactions, communications, and business operations may be crucial evidence. Appropriate documentation can show that the company was abiding by the law and best practices.

4. Risk Management Practices: You can greatly lower the possibility of litigation or claims against your company by implementing thorough risk management procedures, such as personnel training, safety procedures, and adherence to industry norms.

5. Speak with Legal Experts: Seeking advice from legal experts regularly will help you see any hazards and make sure your company complies with legal requirements. Contract drafting, liability advice, and overcoming legal obstacles are all tasks that a lawyer may help with.

One of the main advantages of creating an LLC is the protection of assets and liability. However, making the LLC alone is not enough to provide this protection. LLC owners can greatly lower their liability risk by adhering to the correct legal procedures, keeping personal and corporate assets clearly segregated, obtaining the appropriate insurance, and drafting a thorough operating agreement. Furthermore, you can confidently operate your LLC, knowing that your personal and corporate assets are protected if you comprehend the fundamentals of shielding your company from litigation and claims.

You may optimize the advantages of your LLC while lowering risks and guaranteeing long-term success by using these proactive measures.

CHAPTER 5: FINANCIAL MANAGEMENT FOR YOUR LLC

In addition to maintaining tax compliance, managing your LLC's funds well is crucial for your company's long-term expansion and prosperity. Managing income, keeping tabs on spending, and keeping correct documents are all your responsibilities as an LLC owner. This chapter will cover several tactics and best practices for handling the finances of your LLC, such as creating corporate bank accounts, separating personal and business funds, building credit, and choosing the appropriate financial instruments for your company. Additionally, we will discuss the significance of correct bookkeeping and accounting for legal compliance and your own peace of mind.

CREATING BANK ACCOUNTS FOR BUSINESSES

Establishing a company bank account is one of the first stages in handling the money of your LLC. Maintaining clear financial records, preserving your personal assets, and ensuring that your tax returns are accurate all depend on this fundamental practice of keeping your personal and business finances apart.

When you set up a business bank account, you need to ensure the following:

1. Separate Personal and Business Transactions: By opening a business account, you prevent personal expenses from mingling with your business transactions, which makes tax reporting easier and ensures that your LLC's finances are transparent.

2. Proper Documentation: You'll need certain documents to open a business account, including:

Your LLC's **Articles of Organization**

- **Employer Identification Number (EIN)** from the IRS
- Operating Agreement (if applicable)

3. Choosing the Right Bank: Different banks offer various services for LLCs, such as business loans, credit lines, and merchant services. When selecting a bank, look for one that provides:

- Low fees
- Easy access to online banking
- A broad range of business services

Having a business bank account is critical for your LLC's legal structure, as it helps to reinforce the distinction between personal and business liabilities.

HOW TO MAINTAIN FINANCIAL DISTINCTION BETWEEN PERSONAL AND BUSINESS

For any LLC owner, keeping personal and corporate finances apart is essential. Combining individual and business funds can lead to financial, tax, and legal issues. When it comes to safeguarding your own possessions, this is particularly crucial.

Here's how to get a distinct separation:

1. **Create a Dedicated Business Bank Account:** As previously said, the first step in keeping your personal and business finances apart is to create a dedicated business account. Only business income, spending, and transactions should be made using this account.

2. **Create a company Credit Card:** Using a different business credit card ensures keeping personal and company expenses apart. It also enables you to establish company credit.

3. **Refrain from Using Personal Money for Business Expenses:** Although it could be alluring to make business purchases using your credit card, it can be difficult to distinguish between your personal and business expenses. Rather, for LLC-related transactions, always use your business credit lines and accounts.

4. **Monitor Every Transaction:** Track business revenue and expenses using accounting software or hiring a qualified accountant. This makes it easier to keep business-related and personal interactions separate.

Maintaining financial segregation is essential for liability protection as well as taxation. Keeping your funds separate helps shield your personal assets from being targeted by creditors or lawsuits should you ever face legal problems.

OVERVIEW OF BUSINESS CREDIT: HOW TO BUILD YOUR LLC'S CREDIT

Establishing business credit is essential to your LLC's long-term financial stability. Building up your company's credit can help you get financing, get approved for business loans, and negotiate good terms with suppliers and vendors. However, building company credit is not the same as building personal credit.

The following are the essential actions to build your LLC's credit:

1. Acquire an EIN (Employer Identification Number): For tax reasons, this nine-digit IRS-issued number is your LLC's "social security number." Building business credit and opening accounts in your company's name requires it.

2. Sign up with agencies that report business credit: Business credit scores are similar to those of individuals. The credit history of your LLC is monitored by the main business credit reporting agencies, including Equifax Business, Experian Business, and Dun & Bradstreet.

3. Create Trade Credit: Many merchants and suppliers will give you terms like "net 30" or "net 60," which provides you with 30 or 60 days to settle your invoice. Your company can start building a good credit history by making timely payments on these bills.

4. Apply for a business credit card: Once your LLC has obtained its EIN and built up some trade credit, apply for a business credit card in your company's name. To prevent interest and establish credit, utilize it sensibly and pay off the remaining monthly amount.

5. Keep Up a Good Payment History: A history of on-time payments is the foundation of corporate credit, just like personal credit. Since late payments can seriously harm your LLC's credit score, be careful to pay all bills and debts on schedule.

Although it takes time, establishing company credit is essential to your LLC's expansion and financial health.

SELECTING AN APPROPRIATE BUSINESS CREDIT CARD

A business credit card is an essential financial tool for LLCs, allowing you to manage expenses and build your business's credit profile. When choosing a business credit card, consider the following:

Benefits of Using a Business Credit Card:

1. Separation of Expenses: A business credit card helps keep business expenses separate from personal ones, which is crucial for tax reporting and legal purposes.

2. Rewards and Perks: Many business credit cards offer rewards, such as cashback, travel points, or discounts on business-related purchases.

3. Establishing Business Credit: By using a business credit card responsibly, you build your LLC's credit history, which will make it easier to secure loans and favorable terms with suppliers.

HOW TO BUILD BUSINESS CREDIT WITH CREDIT CARDS:

1. Make On-Time Payments: Ensure you pay your credit card bill on time each month. Timely payments will improve your business credit score and strengthen your reputation with creditors.

2. Keep Utilization Low: Avoid maxing out your credit card. A low utilization ratio (the amount of credit you use relative to your credit limit) helps build a positive credit history.

Maximizing Rewards While Managing Expenses:

1. Track Expenses: Use your business credit card to pay for everyday business expenses. Set up notifications to track spending and stay within budget.

2. Choose the Right Card for Your Business: Look for cards that offer rewards aligned with your business's needs, such as office supplies, travel, or online marketing expenses.

MAINTAINING PRECISE FINANCIAL DOCUMENTS

Maintaining accurate financial records is crucial to your LLC's efficient functioning. They support you in adhering to tax regulations, being ready for audits, and making wise choices for your company's future. The following information will help you keep accurate financial records for your LLC:

1. Monitor Earnings and Outlays: Regularly log all your earnings and business-related outlays. Accounting programs that automatically sync transactions from your bank and credit accounts, such as FreshBooks or QuickBooks, can make this process easier.

2. Different Tax Accounts: Create a different account to hold money for your tax liabilities. Doing this may prevent fines and ensure you have enough money to pay your taxes on time each quarter.

3. Preserve Documents for Tax Deductions: Preserve records and receipts for all deductible company expenses, including marketing expenditures, office supplies, and travel expenses. Your taxable income will be lowered as a result.

EVERYTHING YOU SHOULD KNOW ABOUT LLC BOOKKEEPING AND ACCOUNTING

Bookkeeping and accounting are essential parts of running your LLC's finances. The following are the main things you should be aware of:

1. Accounting Systems: An accounting system in place is crucial, regardless of whether you handle your accounts professionally or independently. Use accounting software to monitor your financial activity or work with a certified public accountant (CPA).

2. Financial Declarations: Pay attention to your LLC's cash flow, income, and balance sheets. These records offer a quick overview of your company's financial decision-making.

3. Hiring a Professional: To guarantee that your records are accurate and your taxes are filed correctly, it could be prudent to engage a professional if you are unfamiliar with accounting principles.

You can make sure that your LLC's finances are in order and prepared for any obstacles that may come up by maintaining organization, employing the appropriate tools, and maintaining thorough records. Growth and success depend on effective financial management.

Any successful LLC must have strong financial management. Your LLC will be stronger for long-term stability and growth if you set up the right accounts, build business credit, and keep accurate financial records.

CHAPTER 6: STRATEGIES FOR EXPANDING YOUR LLC

Growth is one of your main objectives as a business owner. Increased profitability, a greater market position, and more revenues might result from scaling your LLC successfully. However, growth needs to be carefully planned, strategic, and carried out to prevent overstretching your resources or diverting your attention from key business principles. This chapter will examine the different growth techniques that LLC owners can employ in 2025, emphasizing when and how to scale and the crucial choices about employment, cash flow management, and taking advantage of new market opportunities. We will also review the advantages and disadvantages of joint ventures and partnerships, which can be effective growth vehicles.

SCALING YOUR LLC: HOW AND WHEN TO EXPAND

It's critical to understand when and how to scale your LLC.

Scaling is more than just expanding your company's size; it's about deliberately growing it to optimize sustainability and long-term success. Knowing the phases of expansion your company will experience and the telltale signs that it's time to scale is crucial.

Before jumping, evaluate the following:

1. Stable Cash Flow: To support your expansion initiatives, your company needs to have steady sources of income. Growing your company too quickly could put it in danger of bankruptcy if your cash flow is unpredictable.

2. Developed Procedures and Systems: Effective mechanisms are essential to scaling successfully. Scaling can only worsen inefficiencies if your internal procedures — like order fulfilment, inventory control, and customer service — are not well-established.

3. Sufficient Demand: Verify that your product or service has enough market demand to support growth. Conduct market research to determine whether growing is sustainable and to learn about the wider demand for your products.

Increasing your product options, reaching a wider audience, or stepping up your marketing efforts are some strategies for scaling. Growing your workforce or operations to accommodate the expansion is another essential increasing component. For instance, you could need to recruit more staff to manage the increasing workload or invest in technology to improve company operations.

HIRING WORKERS VS. CONTRACTING OUT

Whether to hire staff or contract out work to independent contractors is a crucial choice when growing your LLC. Employing full-time staff enables you to create a team committed to your business, guaranteeing continuity, loyalty, and an in-depth understanding of your company culture. Both options have benefits and drawbacks, and the choice will be based on your company's needs, budget, and business type. Additionally, full-time staff members can aid in creating long-term plans and eventually support the company's expansion. However, employing people comes with a big price tag regarding wages, benefits, and legal requirements, including payroll taxes, insurance, and labor law compliance.

If you require long-term assistance in key areas of your organization, think about adding staff as you scale. For instance, if sales, customer service, or administrative personnel are essential to the expansion of your company, you may need to hire them.

2. Outsourcing: Outsourcing employs independent contractors or outside service providers to carry out particular duties without hiring them as staff members. With this strategy, you can hire contractors as needed without committing to long-term commitments, giving you flexibility. Outsourcing is frequently the best option for jobs like accounting, marketing, IT support, and legal services.

Because you usually only pay for the services you require, outsourcing has several advantages, one of which is cost savings. Furthermore, outsourcing enables you to access specialist expertise that might not be available internally, freeing you up to concentrate on strategic business expansion.

Consider your long-term business requirements when choosing between outsourcing and recruiting staff. Hiring might be ideal if you need continuous employment supporting your business's strategic goals. Outsourcing can offer cost-effectiveness and flexibility for specialized, seasonal, or temporary tasks.

MANAGING PROFIT MARGINS AND CASH FLOW

Growing your LLC requires efficient cash flow management.

Your company's cash flow is essential to its ability to pay personnel, meet its responsibilities, and reinvest in expansion. Cash flow management is more difficult as your company grows but becomes more crucial.

1. Cash Flow Forecasting: Precise cash flow forecasts enable you to anticipate future financial requirements, account for seasonal fluctuations in income, and make well-informed choices on investments and expenditures. Make thorough cash flow projections using software tools, considering anticipated revenues, operational costs, and capital expenditures.

2. Managing Working Capital: The amount of money accessible for daily operations is known as working capital. As your company grows, make sure it keeps a sufficient amount of operating cash. This will assist you in meeting short-term costs without endangering your expansion goals.

3. Optimizing Profit Margins: As your company expands, concentrate on raising your profit margins by cutting back on wasteful spending, negotiating better terms with suppliers, and streamlining your operations. Keep a careful eye on your operating costs and cost of goods sold (COGS). Over time, little changes in these areas can lead to notable profit increases.

4. Strategic Investments: It's critical to priorities investments that will provide the biggest return while scaling. For instance, purchasing technology that automates monotonous operations can free up resources for more worthwhile endeavors. Additionally, think about spending money on marketing, which might draw in new clients and hasten the expansion of your company.

ENTERING NEW MARKETS

Entering new markets is one of the best strategies to grow your LLC. Market expansion necessitates careful preparation, whether expanding your geographic reach, focusing on new demographics, or changing your product offerings.

1. Market Research: To comprehend the requirements, habits, and preferences of potential clients, carry out in-depth market research before entering a new market. Consider market size, competition, demand, and possible entry barriers. By being aware of these characteristics, you may create an expansion strategy that appeals to your target audience.

2. Approach to Entry: Select the entrance approach that works best for your company. This could entail opening more sites, collaborating with nearby companies, selling online, or obtaining a product license. Your resources, the type of product or service you offer, and the new market's regulatory landscape will all influence the optimal strategy.

3. Modifying Your Products: Modifying them to accommodate local tastes when entering a new market is critical. For instance, if you're going global, consider changing your marketing or products to suit regional preferences, cultural variances, and consumer behavior.

MAKING THE MOST OF JOINT VENTURES AND PARTNERSHIPS

Joint ventures and strategic alliances can effectively grow your LLC without taking on all the expenses and risks by yourself. Working with other companies or entrepreneurs allows you to use their networks, resources, and experience to spur growth.

1. Selecting the Correct Partners: When considering joint ventures, seek out companies or people whose skills align with yours. Ensure the collaboration fits your client base, values, and company objectives. For instance, you can lower operating expenses or increase your reach by collaborating with a distributor or supplier.

2. Collaborative Projects: A more official cooperation that frequently entails shared ownership and earnings is called a joint venture (JV). You can more effectively obtain financing through joint ventures, develop new goods, or investigate new markets. To avoid future misunderstandings, make sure that the JV's terms are precisely stated in a formal contract.

3. Handling Partnership Risks: Partnerships may be risky, particularly if management philosophies, corporate objectives, or operational capacities diverge. Establish clear agreements, communicate honestly with your partners, and ensure that everyone is equally involved in the venture's success to reduce risks.

It takes careful planning, smart thinking, and knowledge of the various growth paths to scale your LLC. You may boost your company's reach and profitability by controlling cash flow, entering new markets, and utilizing partnerships. Always think about your long-term objectives and ensure that any expansion initiatives align with your company's basic values, whether you decide to outsource or hire staff. Continue honing your tactics as your company expands to maintain your competitive edge and attain long-term success.

CHAPTER 7: LLC COMPLIANCE AND ONGOING MAINTENANCE

You have additional obligations after your LLC is formed. Keeping your LLC in good standing is crucial to safeguarding the advantages and legal protections it provides, such as restricted liability. Maintaining current and correct records and adhering to state and federal regulations are essential for preventing fines, legal problems, or the possible closure of your company. The ongoing compliance obligations that every LLC owner needs to understand are covered in this chapter. These obligations include state-specific regulations, annual reports and fees, the significance of maintaining your LLC's good standing, updating your operating agreement, and what to do if your LLC is dissolved or terminated.

ANNUAL REPORTING AND FEES

Many states require you to submit annual or biennial reports to the Secretary of State or another designated entity after your LLC has been successfully created. These reports are intended to verify your LLC's present state and update you on any modifications to your company. The names of the LLC members, the registered agent's details, the company address, and any other information required to maintain your records current may be among the data asked.

The Significance of Annual Reports

Annual reports serve two purposes: they keep your LLC compliant with state laws and business operations transparent. Most states demand these filings to ensure that companies operating within their borders are legitimate and operational. If these reports are not filed on time, your LLC may be dissolved or subject to fines and penalties.

Annual Charges

In addition to filing an annual report, most states impose a fee for maintaining the good standing of your LLC. Depending on the state, the fee might cost anything from $50 to $800 annually. California, for instance, has an annual franchise tax of $800, but Delaware allows LLCs to pay as little as $300, depending on your business's operations. To be sure you are budgeting for this ongoing cost, keep an eye on your state's charge schedule.

You can still pay these fees if your company isn't making enough money in a certain year. If you fail to comply, your LLC may be suspended or dissolved by the state.

STATE-SPECIFIC LLC COMPLIANCE STANDARDS

The standards for LLC compliance vary from state to state. The state in which your LLC is founded or operated determines a large portion of the regulatory environment, even while there are federal regulations that regulate some parts of LLC operations, such as tax reporting and employment obligations.

State-Specific Regulations You Must Understand

1. Registered Agent Requirement: In practically all states, LLCs must designate a registered agent, a person or organization accepting official communications and legal papers on the LLC's behalf. If your company is growing in more than one state, you might need to choose a registered agent in each state.

2. State Taxes and Fees: LLCs are subject to various tax regimes in different states. While some, like California, have significant franchise taxes, others, like South Dakota and Wyoming, have no state income tax. Your tax requirements are influenced by your LLC's structure, location, and revenue. To prevent unforeseen costs, it is essential to comprehend these state-specific taxes.

3. Annual Franchise Taxes: LLCs must pay an annual franchise tax in several states, including Delaware and California. This is a fee to conduct your business in the state, not a tax on your income. While some governments impose a fixed fee, others base the franchise tax on revenue or income.

4. Status of Foreign LLC: You might need to register as a foreign LLC in other states if you're doing business outside the state where your LLC was established. Usually, this procedure entails paying extra fees and filing an application to the state where you want to conduct business.

Because state laws can vary, it's critical to determine what your state requires for compliance or get legal advice to ensure your LLC stays in good standing.

HOW TO MAINTAIN THE GOOD STANDING OF YOUR LLC

Preserving your LLC's limited liability protections and avoiding needless fines depend on keeping it in good standing. To make sure your LLC stays in compliance, follow these crucial steps:

1. File Annual Reports on Time: As was previously said, annual reporting is an essential part of LLC compliance. To avoid fines or penalties, submit your report before the deadline.

2. Pay All Necessary Fees: Ensure you understand all the costs involved in maintaining the good standing of your LLC. This covers franchise taxes, state filing fees, and other expenses that may be necessary based on your state.

3. Update the Details of Your LLC: Make sure the information about your LLC is current. If you alter your registered agent, members, or company address, submit the required paperwork to your state to update your LLC's records. Failure to do so may result in penalties, dissolution, or missed legal paperwork.

4. Keep Correct Business documents: Maintaining accurate records is crucial for your LLC's integrity and tax purposes. Ensure your company conforms with any licensing or regulatory requirements, that your financial records are well-organized, and that your contracts are current.

UPDATING YOUR OPERATING AGREEMENT

One of your LLC's most crucial documents is the operating agreement. Although not mandated in all states, it is strongly advised that all LLCs have one. Your LLC's internal organization, including decision-making procedures, profit sharing, and member duties and obligations, is described in the operating agreement.

Your company may evolve regarding operations, ownership, or financial structure over time. To ensure your operating agreement accurately reflects your current business position, examining and amending it regularly is crucial.

Motives for Revising Your Operating Agreement

1. Ownership Changes: The operating agreement should be amended to reflect any changes in ownership that occur within your LLC, whether they are brought about by the departure of existing members, the inclusion of new members, or a transfer of ownership.

2. Changing Business Structure: You might need to modify the management structure specified in the agreement if your company grows or takes a different course. For example, a formal amendment can be necessary if an LLC changes from member-managed to manager-managed.

3. Tax Classification Changes: The operating agreement may need to be amended to reflect any changes you make to your LLC's tax classification, such as moving from a disregarded organization to an S-Corporation.

In addition to keeping your company compliant with legal and operational standards, updating your operating agreement can shield you from member conflicts.

WHAT TO DO IN THE EVENT OF A TERMINATION OR DISSOLUTION OF YOUR LLC

Your LLC may be dissolved freely or unwillingly under specific conditions. Involuntary dissolution can happen if you don't comply with state regulations, including not paying taxes or filing yearly reports, whereas voluntary dissolution happens when the owners elect to close the business.

Dissolution voluntarily

Following the correct procedures is essential if you officially dissolve your LLC. Dissolution entails:

1. Filing Articles of Dissolution: To properly close your LLC, most states require you to submit a formal document known as Articles of Dissolution to the Secretary of State.

2. Resolving Business obligations: You must pay any outstanding business obligations or liabilities before dissolving the LLC. This procedure can entail selling company assets and allocating the remaining funds to the participants.

3. Notifying Clients and Creditors: To ensure that you meet all legal obligations and complete all commitments, it's also critical to inform any clients and creditors that your LLC is dissolving.

Unintentional Dissolution

You might need to take care of these problems before reestablishing your LLC if it was dissolved involuntarily because you didn't pay taxes or file annual reports as required by the state. You could occasionally have to pay fines or back costs to recover your LLC's status.

Your company will be safe and prevent dissolution if you maintain compliance and proactively manage your LLC's legal obligations.

LLC upkeep and compliance are continuous duties that call for prompt action and close attention to detail. You can ensure your firm runs effectively and enjoys the legal protections it offers by adhering to the correct procedures to maintain good standing, updating pertinent papers such as your operating agreement, and being aware of the rules and regulations that apply to your LLC.

CHAPTER 8: 2025 LLC TRENDS AND FUTURE-PROOFING YOUR BUSINESS

The business world is always changing, and to be competitive and ensure their company succeeds in the years to come, LLC owners need to keep up with new trends and laws. New trends are changing how LLCs function as the mid-2020s draw near, and technology is becoming a more important factor in how companies are set up, run, and grow. The main themes that LLC owners should be aware of in 2025 and beyond, how technology is changing the LLC landscape, how to adjust to shifting company regulations and tax laws, and tactics for maintaining your LLC's competitiveness in the digital era are all covered in this chapter.

NEW DEVELOPMENTS FOR LLCS IN 2025 AND LATER

The future of LLCs is shaped by several significant themes as we move into 2025. Rapid technical breakthroughs, changing consumer habits, and changing economic conditions are the causes of these changes. Long-term success depends on your ability to comprehend and adjust to these patterns. Let's examine some of the most important developments that LLC owners should be aware of in more detail:

1. Remote Work and Digital Transformation

The trend toward remote work was driven by the COVID-19 epidemic and is predicted to continue in the years to come. LLCs are increasingly implementing hybrid or totally remote company models to increase recruiting flexibility, save overhead costs, and reach a wider audience. LLCs can function effectively across several locations thanks to the ongoing development of cloud computing, virtual collaboration tools, and video conferencing systems.

Businesses are adopting remote work and digital transformation, which is integrating digital technologies into every aspect of operations. For LLCs, this entails using project management, accounting, marketing, and customer relationship management (CRM) software to increase productivity and streamline processes. By embracing digital tools, LLC owners may improve customer service, make better decisions, and save time and money.

2. Social responsibility and sustainability

Consumers are giving sustainability, moral behavior, and corporate social responsibility (CSR) more weight when purchasing. By incorporating sustainable practices into their business models—whether through energy-efficient operations, ecologically friendly products, or ethical sourcing and production methods—LLCs are anticipated to contribute to this trend.

LLCs will likely acquire a competitive edge, increase their consumer base, and strengthen brand loyalty if they implement sustainable practices and show their dedication to social responsibility. Furthermore, companies that put sustainability first frequently receive grants, tax breaks, and other government assistance, making it a wise and profitable long-term growth plan.

3. A greater emphasis on cybersecurity and data privacy

Businesses of all sizes must proactively safeguard their sensitive data as cybersecurity threats increase and data breaches become more frequent. To protect consumer data, financial information, and intellectual property, LLC owners should be ready to invest significantly in cybersecurity.

LLCs must abide by the General Data Protection Regulation (GDPR) and other privacy legislation prioritizing consumer data protection. LLC owners must prioritize compliance and put best practices into place to ensure they fulfil ethical and legal standards for data protection, as the trend of increased concern over data privacy is expected to continue in 2025 and beyond.

HOW THE LLC LANDSCAPE IS BEING SHAPED BY TECHNOLOGY

One of the most significant developments of the last ten years has been using technology in corporate operations, which is still changing the LLC scene. Among the many advantages of technology are enhanced productivity, better client experiences, and new business prospects. Knowing how to use technology as an LLC owner can help you differentiate your company from rivals and keep it flexible in a constantly evolving market.

1. Cloud computing

Instead of depending on physical servers or infrastructure, cloud computing enables LLCs to store data and operate applications remotely over the internet. Businesses can now more easily scale rapidly, access critical information from any location, and cut operating expenses. Cloud-based accounting, inventory management, project tracking, and communication technologies are increasingly indispensable for LLCs to maintain efficient operations and promote teamwork across geographical boundaries.

2. Artificial Intelligence (AI) and Automation

The way LLCs manage repetitive tasks like data analysis, marketing campaigns, and customer service inquiries is changing due to automation tools and artificial intelligence. For instance, chatbots can respond to consumer inquiries around the clock, enabling companies to improve customer service without hiring more employees. Similarly, AI-driven marketing solutions may evaluate customer behavior and automatically modify ad campaigns to maximize results, saving LLC owners time and money.

Finance and accounting are likewise heavily reliant on automation. With the help of programs like Xero and QuickBooks, business owners can easily create financial reports, track spending, and automate invoicing. This helps guarantee that financial management complies with current tax rules and regulations while increasing accuracy.

3. Online sales and e-commerce

LLCs have been significantly impacted by the growth of e-commerce, particularly those in the industrial, retail, and service sectors. LLCs must adjust by making the most of their internet presence, as online sales are expected to keep increasing. This entails creating an online store, putting safe payment systems in place, and ensuring that customers can easily shop on all devices.

Social commerce, or the direct sale of goods via social media platforms, has become increasingly popular in addition to traditional e-commerce. Many LLCs increasingly use Facebook and Instagram in their sales plans to reach a larger audience and increase income through social media channels4. Cryptocurrency and Blockchain

Although they are still in their infancy, blockchain technology and cryptocurrencies have drawn much attention recently and offer LLCs a special chance to be creative. For instance, the decentralized nature of blockchain can assist LLCs in increasing transparency, decreasing fraud, and streamlining supply chain management.

Accepting cryptocurrencies as payment could also draw in tech-savvy clients who favor digital currencies and provide new revenue sources. LLCs must remain aware of the legal ramifications of utilizing blockchain technology and taking Bitcoin payments as cryptocurrency regulations continue to change.

ADAPTING TO CHANGING TAX LAWS AND BUSINESS REGULATIONS

The business regulatory environment is ever-evolving. LLCs must keep up with employment rules, tax laws, and other legal obligations to maintain compliance and prevent expensive errors. LLCs will be impacted by several significant changes to business regulations and tax laws in 2025; you must comprehend these changes to prepare your company for the future.

1. Pass-Through Taxation Changes

The pass-through taxation structure of an LLC, in which gains and losses are distributed to the owners and recorded on their individual tax returns, is one of its main advantages. However, the implementation of pass-through taxation may be impacted by changes to tax legislation in 2025. Any changes to tax rates, credits, and deductions that may affect their personal tax obligations should be communicated to LLC owners.

2. A Closer Examination of LLCs in Specific Sectors

Regulators are paying more attention to certain industries, such as technology, healthcare, and financial services. LLCs operating in these industries can be subject to more frequent audits, stronger reporting guidelines, and increased compliance obligations. Avoiding fines and penalties requires keeping up with industry-specific laws and legal developments.

3. Modifications to the Rules and Deduction Limits

Some changes to company deductions brought about by the 2017 Tax Cuts and Jobs Act (TCJA) are anticipated to be repeated in 2025. LLC owners must know the most recent deduction caps for business expenses, including equipment acquisitions, staff salaries, and perks. Maximizing tax savings can also be achieved by comprehending how deductions relate to your LLC's business structure.

KEEPING YOUR LLC COMPETITIVE IN A DIGITAL AGE

For LLCs, the digital era offers both possibilities and difficulties. Technology makes it possible for LLCs to grow and reach a worldwide audience, but it also makes competition fiercer than before. LLC owners must embrace innovation, use data, and constantly adjust their company plans to remain competitive.

1. Making Decisions Based on Data

Data is one of the most important resources a company may have in the digital age. LLCs can make well-informed decisions on product development, marketing tactics, and expansion plans by utilizing market research, sales analytics, and customer data. LLCs can obtain a competitive edge and make strategic decisions based on real-time insights by investing in data collecting and analysis technologies.

2. Strategies for Customer-Centric Marketing

Due to the transition to digital platforms, LLCs must concentrate on providing individualized, customer-centric experiences. LLCs can customize their marketing campaigns to target particular client segments with pertinent offers and content by utilizing data from social media, customer feedback, and purchase behavior. LLCs can improve customer loyalty and forge closer ties with clients by using technologies like customer relationship management (CRM) software.

3. Flexibility and Adaptability

Adaptability is the key to remaining competitive in a corporate climate that is changing quickly. Long-term success is more likely for LLCs that can quickly adapt to new trends, technology, or changes in the economy. LLCs must remain adaptable and ready to change, whether embracing newer technologies, switching to e-commerce or implementing new marketing strategies.

Staying ahead of the curve, adopting new technologies, and being flexible in shifting market conditions and tax regulations are all necessary to future-proof your LLC. LLC owners will set themselves up for long-term growth and success in an increasingly competitive and digital business environment if they monitor new prospects and ensure compliance with changing legislation as we move into 2025 and beyond.

CHAPTER 9: A COMPREHENSIVE GUIDE TO LLC FORMATION.

One of the most crucial phases in starting a business is forming a Limited Liability Company (LLC). An LLC offers tax advantages, permits different management arrangements, and safeguards personal assets. However, creating an LLC may be challenging if you know the administrative and legal requirements. This chapter will review the steps needed to incorporate your LLC, ensuring you comprehend each one. From selecting your state to finishing the necessary paperwork and obtaining the required licenses, we will guide you through the procedure.

First Step: Choose a Name for Your LLC

Selecting a name for your company is the first step in forming an LLC. The name you choose will represent your company and play a significant role in its corporate identity. However, creating an LLC involves more than just selecting a name you like; it also needs to adhere to specific legal regulations.

- Verify that the name of your LLC is distinct in the state where you filed. To find out if your chosen name has already been used, consult the business name database in your state.

- Add the necessary terms: The phrase "Limited Liability Company" or an acronym like "LLC" or "L.L.C." must be in the name of your LLC. This criterion ensures that anyone with your company knows its limitations and structure.

- Steer clear of restricted words: To be used in your LLC name, some terms, such as "bank," "insurance," or "trust," can require further approvals or licenses. To prevent choosing prohibited terms, check the regulations in your state.

- Think about registering your final name as a trademark. This shields your brand from misunderstanding or legal issues by preventing other businesses from utilizing the same name in the future.

Step 2: Decide on Your Formation State

Although you would think that establishing an LLC in your home state is your only choice, many entrepreneurs would rather do it in a different state with more favorable tax and legal regulations. It's important to research which state is best for your company because each has various rules and expenses.

- Home State Formation: To expedite the process, you should incorporate your LLC if you intend to conduct most of your business in your home state. Your LLC will be categorized as a "domestic" LLC in that state.

- International LLCs: Delaware and Nevada are popular states for LLC formation because they have business-friendly laws, appealing tax laws, and robust privacy protections. If you incorporate your LLC in another state, register it as a "foreign" LLC in your home state and any additional states where you do business. However, you might have to pay extra taxes and fees if most of your firm is run in a different state.

Step 3: Designate a Registered Representative

The law requires all LLCs to select a Registered Agent. Legal documents, including tax notices and lawsuits, are sent to the registered agent on behalf of the LLC. The agent needs to be available during business hours and have a physical address in the state where your LLC is registered.

- Who Is Eligible for Registration as an Agent? A company offering registered agent services or a person can be considered a registered agent. You can act as your own registered agent if you do business in your home state, but many entrepreneurs would rather work with a professional registered agent to ensure privacy and compliance.

- Expert Services for Registered Agents: These services offer extra features like privacy, compliance tracking, and document forwarding, but they usually come with an annual subscription.

Step 4: Submit the Organization's Articles

The Articles of Organization, sometimes called a Certificate of Formation, must next be submitted to the Secretary of State in your state to create an LLC. This document includes your company's name, address, and registered agent, among other essential details.

- You'll need: Typically, you need the following details when filing:

Provide your LLC's name, primary address, and registered agent details.

The management structure of an LLC (managers or members) The objective of an LLC (brief description of company activities)

- Filing costs: There is usually a fee to file the organization's articles, which differs from state to state. This can be anything from $50 to $500, depending on where you file.

Step 5: Draft and approve an operating agreement.

It is strongly advised that you create an Operating Agreement for your LLC, even if it is not required in many states. This legal document outlines the ownership structure and operational protocols of your business. Having an operating agreement is essential for preventing misunderstandings and guaranteeing the smooth operation of your company, even if your state does not require one.

- An operating agreement's contents: Typically, the deal specifies: - The percentage of member ownership, Distribution of profit and loss, Decision-making processes, LLC management (managers or members), procedures for adding and removing members, and Procedures for dissolution.

- Why it matters: Without an operating agreement, your LLC can be governed by default state laws that don't reflect your intentions or goals. It is particularly crucial when the LLC has multiple members.

Obtain an Employer Identification Number (EIN) in step six.

An Employer Identification Number (EIN) and a Federal Tax Identification Number are necessary for most LLCs. For tax purposes, the IRS uses this number to identify your company. Employing employees, opening a business bank account, and filing taxes all require it.

- How to apply: The IRS website allows you to apply for an EIN and get a quick confirmation. You may get an EIN right away, and the process is free.

- You need to get an EIN if your LLC has a large membership or intends to hire employees. If you plan to create a business bank account or submit certain tax forms, you might need one, even if you are a single-member LLC.

Step 7: File your local and state taxes.

You might need to register for different state and municipal taxes, depending on your location and type of business. Sales tax, usage tax, unemployment insurance tax, and so on are examples of this.

• Sales and Use Tax: In most states, LLCs that sell physical goods must collect sales tax from clients. The tax department in your state is where you must submit an application for a sales tax permit.

• Employment taxes: Register for state unemployment insurance (SUI) and withhold taxes if you plan to hire employees. These levies guarantee that state taxes are subtracted from employee paychecks and sustain unemployment benefits.

Step 8: Adhere to Additional Licenses and Permits

Many businesses require additional permissions or licenses to operate legally and file taxes. These can include professional licenses in law, medicine, and finance, as well as health permits for businesses involved in the food industry.

- Depending on the state or local jurisdiction and the type of business, different business licenses may be required. These must be current and are issued by state or local governments.

- Permits specific to a given industry: Some sectors, like construction, food service, and healthcare, usually call for particular regulatory licenses or certificates.

Step 9: Comply with continuing legal and regulatory obligations.

To maintain your LLC's good standing, you must continue to fulfil your legal and regulatory obligations. This entails filing yearly reports, paying applicable fees, and keeping up-to-date registered agent information.

- The majority of states mandate that LLCs submit reports every year or every two years that include updated contact details and business status. Failure to submit this report could lead to fines or your LLC being dissolved.

- State fees: Maintaining your LLC's registration requires an annual charge in many states. This fee ranges from $50 to over $500 per year, with significant variations per state.

Step 10: Keep abreast of modifications to compliance.

Lastly, monitor any changes to federal or state regulations

affecting your LLC. Your company's structure or operations may need to alter in response to modifications in tax laws, corporate rules, or industry-specific needs. Consulting with a tax or legal expert guarantees that your LLC is compliant and clear of needless dangers.

By following these ten steps, you may effectively incorporate your LLC and make sure your business is compliant with the law, financially secure, and positioned for long-term success. Even though the process could seem overwhelming at first, each phase offers vital safeguards and benefits to support your company's success.

BONUS CONTENTS

1. INSURANCE GUIDELINES FOR LLC OWNERS.

When you own a Limited Liability Company (LLC), one of the most important components of running your business is ensuring that it is appropriately secured from risks and calamities that you could not have ever anticipated. By separating the shareholders' personal assets from the firm's duties, a limited liability company (LLC) provides legal protection for its shareholders but does not shield the organization from all possible liabilities. Accidents, lawsuits, damage to property, and injuries sustained by employees are examples of situations that could negatively impact the LLC's finances. This is why having insurance for your company is so important.

Insurance for limited liability companies (LLCs) acts as a safety net, protecting the company and its owners from the financial repercussions that may result from the risks that they face. In this lesson, we will discuss the various forms of insurance that owners of limited liability companies (LLCs) ought to take into consideration, the reasons why each type of insurance is essential to their company, and how having the appropriate coverage may be beneficial to the long-term viability of your LLC.

Insurance options for LLC owners:

The owner of a limited liability company (LLC) must investigate several insurance options to guarantee that the company is adequately protected. There may be variations in the specific rules you need to follow based on your company's sector, location, and size. These are the most frequent types of company insurance that owners of limited liability companies (LLCs) should consider purchasing.

1. General Liability Insurance.

General Liability Insurance, sometimes called GLI, is the commercial insurance most frequently associated with small and medium-sized firms. Because it offers protection against various dangers, it is an essential investment for most limited liability organizations. By purchasing this insurance, your company will be protected against claims of bodily harm,

property damage, and complaints against advertising or personal injury complaints.

- The coverage that it provides includes legal bills, settlements, and judgments that are incurred due to incidents on your property or as a consequence of the products or services you provide. For example, this coverage will help pay for legal fees and settlements if a customer slips and falls while shopping at your establishment or if a product that you sell causes harm to a consumer.

- Why it is important: As a limited liability company (LLC) owner, you want to shield your company against litigation that could financially wreck it. General liability insurance is typically required when getting into contracts with consumers, landlords, or companies that provide goods or services. It is not only beneficial to the financial health of your company, but it also helps to develop trust with both your consumers and your business partners.

2. Professional Liability Insurance (Errors And Omissions Coverage)

Consider purchasing Professional Liability Insurance (Errors and Omissions Insurance) if your limited liability company (LLC) offers professional services or advice. Your business is safeguarded by this insurance policy if a client files a lawsuit against you for errors, negligence, or bad services that result in monetary loss.

Expenses for legal defense and settlements for errors or omissions in the services provided by your organization are covered by professional liability insurance. In particular, this is of the utmost importance for service-based organizations such as consultants, accountants, attorneys, architects, and others whose advice or conduct may be contested. Reasons why it is essential: Because of the litigious nature of today's culture, even the smallest mistakes or missed deadlines could result in expensive legal action. The presence of professional liability insurance guarantees that your business will be able to deal with these claims without putting its finances in jeopardy. For companies that offer services such as guidance, design, consultation, or other activities in which the failure to satisfy the expectations of customers could result in a financial loss for those customers, it is of the utmost importance.

3. Workers' Compensation Insurance

Workers' compensation insurance will pay for their medical expenses and any lost wages when an employee is injured or unwell. In most states, firms with employees are required to have workers' compensation, but the specific regulations differ from state to state.

- The insurance coverage will pay for medical expenditures, rehabilitation fees, and lost wages due to work-related illnesses or accidents. The policy may pay for funeral expenses and provide death benefits to the family if an employee dies due to a disease or injury. What makes it so valuable? Your employees will be protected by workers' compensation insurance, and your company will be able to demonstrate compliance with state regulations. Additionally, it helps preserve your limited liability company against lawsuits brought about by injuries that occur on the job. If you do not have sufficient coverage, you run the danger of being held personally responsible for accidents on the job, which may lead to highly expensive legal fights and damage to your reputation.

4. Property insurance.

The tangible assets of your firm, such as buildings, equipment, inventory, and furniture, are safeguarded by your company's property insurance. This cannot be overstated for companies operating with pricey machinery or possessing considerable physical assets.

- What it includes is: In addition to protecting your property from natural catastrophes (such as storms and floods), property insurance protects it from theft, vandalism, and flames. In addition to safeguarding merchandise, it can protect buildings, office equipment, and computers. What makes it so valuable? You should purchase property insurance if your company depends on physical space or pricey equipment. Without this coverage, your limited liability company (LLC) could suffer substantial financial losses due to theft, fire, or natural disasters, which could significantly influence its ability to function and even force it to stop down temporarily or permanently.

5. Business Interruption Insurance.

If your company is forced to temporarily close its doors due to a covered event, such as a fire or a natural disaster, business interruption insurance, also commonly referred to as business income insurance, will protect you against experiencing a loss of income.

- What It Addresses To: This insurance protects your company against financial losses and operational costs incurred due to unanticipated occurrences that take your company out of business. The temporary relocation of your company's operations or the restoration of those operations may also be included. What makes it so valuable? Small and limited liability companies can suffer losses when unexpected shutdowns occur. This type of insurance ensures that your limited liability company (LLC) can continue operating normally even if regular operations are disturbed. Businesses that are vulnerable to natural disasters or rely largely on physical assets to generate revenue especially need this coverage because of its increased importance.

6. Cyber Liability Insurance.

Businesses are increasingly susceptible to cyberattacks, data breaches, and other online risks in this day and age because of the prevalence of digital technology. Cyber Liability Insurance protects your company from various cyber catastrophes like hacking, data leaks, and fraudulent online activity. The expenses associated with data breaches are covered by this policy. These expenses include notification, legal fees, fines, and system repair. Your company's reputation may also be rebuilt with the assistance of public relations operations, which may be covered by this insurance.

- Why is it important to have? The risks associated with cybersecurity are growing, and even small organizations may be susceptible to potential data breaches. Purchasing cyber liability insurance is something you should think about doing if your limited liability company (LLC) deals with sensitive data such as the personal information of customers, financial records, or credit card information. It safeguards against the substantial economic losses that could be incurred due to a cyberattack, which would otherwise result in the failure of a business.

7. Commercial Automobile Insurance

You must obtain Commercial Auto Insurance if your limited liability company (LLC) owns or runs autos for commercial purposes. This insurance protects the automobiles owned by the company, regardless of whether you own them or whether your staff drive their own vehicles.

• Damage that is caused by incidents that involve company-owned vehicles is covered by commercial auto insurance if it is purchased. Moreover, it protects the policyholder against legal responsibility for any losses or injuries resulting from driving for business-related objectives, such as making deliveries or attending meetings. What makes it so valuable? When it comes to company automobiles, using personal auto insurance could potentially lead to complications in the event of an accident. Commercial auto insurance shields your limited liability company (LLC) against the dangers of utilizing automobiles for business purposes. It is important for firms that provide delivery services, mobile businesses, and automotive fleet companies to maintain this.

Why is insurance important for LLC owners

As the owner of a limited liability company (LLC), insurance is not merely a choice; rather, it is essential to the long-term survival of your business. A sufficient amount of insurance coverage is necessary for several reasons, the most important of which are as follows:

1. Legal Protection: In today's litigious world, businesses are constantly at risk of being sued. Legal protection is essential in this environment. Your limited liability company (LLC) may sustain severe financial damages due to legal actions without adequate insurance. Several types of insurance offer protection against these possible dangers. These include general liability insurance, professional liability insurance, and workers' compensation insurance.

2. Protection of Assets: Although a limited liability company (LLC) shields its members from personal liability, the corporation's assets are nevertheless vulnerable to being stolen, damaged, or sued. Your limited liability company (LLC) can continue functioning without incurring irreparable losses if it has business insurance to safeguard its physical assets.

3. **Peace of mind:** running a business comes with its own set of inherent dangers. Comprehensive insurance coverage gives you the peace of mind that comes with knowing that your company is equipped with the financial resources necessary to deal with unforeseen events without jeopardizing its future.

4. **Legal Compliance:** The maintenance of certain forms of insurance, including workers' compensation, is required of limited liability companies (LLCs) with employees. You risk fines and penalties and potentially losing your LLC's good standing with the state if you do not have adequate coverage.

5. **Financial Stability:** Insurance guarantees that your limited liability company (LLC) has the capability to recover from unforeseen catastrophes. If your company does not have coverage, it may have difficulty recovering, lose customers and reputation, or even go out of business.

In the current unpredictable business environment, acquiring sufficient insurance coverage for your limited liability company (LLC) is prudent and essential to ensure your company's future. In addition to general liability insurance, cyber liability insurance is another type of insurance that offers significant protection against threats to your firm's financial stability or reputation. Awareness of the many forms of insurance available enables you to make educated decisions that safeguard your business, your employees, and your personal assets, allowing you to concentrate on securely expanding your limited liability company.

2. BUSINESS MARKETING STRATEGY GUIDE FOR LLCS

Marketing is a key component of growing any business, and for LLC owners, it can be a difficult but necessary task. A well-executed marketing strategy may help you build your brand, attract customers, and ultimately drive commercial success. However, many entrepreneurs, particularly those just starting out, struggle to understand the most effective techniques for promoting their brand, developing meaningful relationships with clients, and standing out in competitive industries. This comprehensive business marketing strategy guide is designed to help LLC owners create an actionable and results-oriented marketing plan that will drive long-term success.

This tutorial will show you how to build a strong brand, create an effective digital marketing strategy, and leverage social media platforms to increase visibility, engage with your target audience, and convert leads into paying customers. Whether you're new to marketing or want to improve your current approaches, the steps below will walk you through creating a systematic marketing plan that aligns with your LLC's goals.

Building Your Brand Is The Cornerstone Of Your Marketing Approach.

Your brand represents your firm. It expresses who you are, what you offer, and why customers should choose you over the competition. Before implementing marketing strategies, it is necessary to establish a strong and consistent brand image.

1. Identify your brand's mission and values.

A clear brand mission can help you convey your purpose to your target audience. Begin by identifying the difficulties your product or service addresses.

- What distinguishes your business from others?
- What ideas do you want your business to embody?

These questions will create the foundation of your brand's messaging, tone, and positioning. For example, your brand may stress sustainability and ethical sourcing if you own an eco-friendly product company. Your objectives and values will shape your content, how you connect with customers, and the causes you support.

2. Design a memorable logo and visual identity.

A visually appealing logo is an essential component of any brand. Your logo should be simple, versatile, and convey your company's ideals. Along with the logo, design a consistent color scheme, typography, and artwork that reflects your brand's message.

To provide your customers with a consistent brand experience, your visual identity will be applied to all marketing materials, such as your website, social media sites, and business cards.

3. Create your brand's voice and messaging.

Your brand's voice is how you communicate with your intended audience and should be consistent across all platforms. Whether writing a blog post email or engaging with customers on social media, your messaging tone and style should reflect your brand's personality.

Consider whether your brand is more formal or casual, funny or serious, authoritative or welcoming. This tone will help you connect with your target audience and earn their trust over time.

Developing A Digital Marketing Strategy: Engaging Your Audience Online

A solid digital marketing strategy is critical for growing your business in today's digital-first world. It allows you to communicate with potential customers, create brand awareness, and boost conversion rates. The following are the important components to consider when building your digital marketing strategy:

1. Build a website that converts.

Your website is typically the first point of contact between your business and prospective customers. It should be visually appealing, user-friendly, and search engine optimized (SEO). Your website should clearly express who you are, what you offer, and how customers can take action (such as purchasing a product, scheduling a service, or contacting you).

Key Features of an Effective Website:

1. Create unambiguous calls-to-action (CTAs) that prompt visitors to take action, such as joining an email list, purchasing a product, or scheduling a consultation.

Ensure your website is mobile-responsive, as more people use the web on mobile devices than ever before.

To maximize conversions, your website's content should solve customer problems, answer questions, and provide value.

2. Search Engine Optimization (SEO).

SEO ranks your website higher in search engine results pages (SERPs). Increased visibility on search engines like Google can drive organic traffic to your website and generate leads without paid advertising.

Basic SEO tactics involve keyword research and incorporating popular search terms into your content.

On-page SEO entails improving meta tags, headers, images, and internal links to increase search engine visibility.

o Material Marketing Publish high-quality, useful content that answers your target audience's questions and needs.

3. Email marketing.

Email marketing is one of the most effective tactics for developing client relationships and increasing sales. A well-executed email marketing campaign can help you engage your target audience, promote special offers, and improve repeat sales.

To build an email marketing list, offer website visitors incentives such as exclusive content, discounts, or free tools. After you've generated a list, segment it based on customer behavior and preferences, and then use personalized email marketing to move leads through the sales funnel.

4. Content marketing.

Content marketing is an effective way to attract, engage, and convert your target audience. Create exceptional content, such as blog pieces, whitepapers, case studies, or videos, to establish your sector authority, acquire the trust of potential clients, and drive traffic to your website.

Concentrate on developing content that addresses your audience's pain points and challenges. For example, if you sell consulting services, you may write blog posts providing practical advice on business growth, leadership, and strategy.

Using Social Media to Attract Customers

Social media channels are a wonderful method to connect with potential customers, showcase your brand's personality, and build an online community. You can increase visitors, leads, and conversions by creating engaging content and promoting meaningful conversations.

1. Choose the Right Social Media Platform.

Not all social media platforms are appropriate for all businesses. It is crucial to choose platforms where your target audience is most active. Instagram and Pinterest, for example, are perfect for visually appealing industries like fashion, cuisine, and leisure.

- LinkedIn is best suited for B2B firms, professional services, and networking.
- Facebook and Twitter are perfect for organizations wishing to connect with many customers.
- Concentrate on platforms relevant to your business's goals and target audience.

2. Provide shareable and interesting material. To increase social media participation, you must produce appealing content. This could include product demos, behind-the-scenes looks, customer testimonials, and industry insights. Use visual elements such as high-quality images and movies to attract attention and encourage interaction.

Live Streaming and Stories: Instagram, Facebook, and YouTube all offer live streaming features, allowing you to communicate with your audience in real-time. Live Q&As,

product launches, and behind-the-scenes streams are all effective ways to personalize your brand and engage followers.

3. Use targeted social media advertisements.

Consider running paid adverts to expand your reach once you've created a social media page. Platforms like Facebook, Instagram, and LinkedIn offer highly targeted advertising options, allowing you to contact certain demographics based on their interests, behaviors, and location.

Begin with a defined aim (e.g., lead generation, brand visibility, or sales), create appealing ad copy, and evaluate your results to optimize future campaigns.

Why is this information useful to LLC owners?

Marketing is essential for LLC owners looking to achieve long-term success and growth. However, many business owners fail to create and implement a successful marketing strategy. Following the approaches outlined in this article will enable LLC owners to systematically develop their brand, implement a comprehensive digital marketing strategy, and effectively leverage social media to widen their reach.

An effective marketing strategy builds awareness and trust among your target audience.

- Increase leads and customer loyalty.
- Stand out from competitors.
- Maximize earnings using cost-effective marketing channels.

With this knowledge and a well-defined action plan, LLC owners can ensure that their companies thrive in competitive markets and continue to grow in the digital age.

3. EXCLUSIVE ACCESS TO A BUSINESS RESOURCE TOOLKIT

As a business owner, particularly within a Limited Liability Company (LLC) structure, you always look for ways to streamline operations, reduce overhead, and maintain a competitive edge in the marketplace. The right set of tools and resources can significantly impact the efficiency and growth of your business. In today's fast-paced business environment, staying on top of the latest software, apps, and technologies is crucial for staying competitive.

This **Exclusive Business Resource Toolkit** is designed to provide you with a curated list of essential tools, resources, and apps tailored specifically for managing and growing your LLC. From project management and communication tools to accounting and marketing software, this toolkit includes discounts on popular business solutions that will save you time, reduce costs, and increase your operational efficiency. Whether you want to automate tasks, enhance collaboration, or optimize your business processes, this guide will help you identify the best resources to support your business goals.

The Value of Using the Right Business Tools

Running an LLC is not just about handling day-to-day operations; it's about ensuring your company is set up to scale, adapt, and compete effectively. One of the easiest ways to optimize your business operations is using the right tools. However, with an overwhelming number of available options on the market, it can be difficult to know where to start. This toolkit helps eliminate the guesswork, giving you access to a collection of tried-and-tested business tools.

Using the right tools can bring several benefits to your business:

Time-saving: Automation and streamlined processes allow you to spend less time on administrative tasks and focus more on growing your business.

Cost reduction: By choosing efficient tools, you can eliminate unnecessary manual processes and reduce the need for additional staff, thus cutting costs.

Scalability: The right tools grow with your business, allowing you to scale operations smoothly without overhauling your systems as your company expands.

Increased productivity: Tools that simplify collaboration, communication, and project management help teams work faster and more efficiently.

Improved decision-making: Many of these tools offer powerful analytics and reporting capabilities, giving you valuable insights into your business's performance and helping you make more informed decisions.

Essential Tools for Managing Your LLC

Here's a breakdown of some key categories of business tools and resources that every LLC owner should consider. This section highlights tools that can assist you with managing your LLC, from accounting and marketing to team collaboration and customer relationship management.

1. Accounting and Financial Management Tools

Effective financial management is critical to the success of your LLC. Proper accounting ensures that you remain compliant with tax regulations and helps you understand your business's economic health.

QuickBooks: QuickBooks remains one of the most widely used accounting tools for small businesses. It allows you to manage invoices, expenses, payroll, and even track your tax liabilities. With integration capabilities to sync with various bank accounts and payment systems, QuickBooks ensures that your financial records are organized and up-to-date.

FreshBooks: For LLCs that provide services, FreshBooks offers an intuitive invoicing and accounting solution that can simplify the financial side of business. With features like time tracking, project management, and client communication, FreshBooks is an excellent tool for service-based businesses.

Xero: Xero is another cloud-based accounting tool that offers easy-to-use financial management features. With a focus on automation, Xero helps businesses save time on bookkeeping and improves accuracy in financial reporting.

2. Project Management and Collaboration Tools

Whether you have a small team or are working with external contractors, efficient project management and collaboration tools are essential for staying organized and productive.

Trello: Trello offers an easy-to-use, visual project management tool that helps you organize tasks, deadlines, and team assignments. With customizable boards and workflows, Trello suits small and large projects, making it a go-to tool for LLC owners managing multiple tasks.

Asana: Asana helps teams stay on track with complex projects. It offers task assignments, calendar views, file sharing, and communication tools — all in one platform. Whether you're working with an internal team or external partners, Asana can help keep everyone aligned and on time.

Slack: Effective communication is crucial for any business. Slack is a real-time messaging platform that allows team conversations, file sharing, and integrations with other business tools. It's particularly useful for remote teams, ensuring smooth communication regardless of location.

3. Customer Relationship Management (CRM) Tools

Maintaining positive relationships with your customers is essential for long-term business success. CRM software helps you manage your customer base, track interactions, and provide better service.

HubSpot CRM: HubSpot is a powerful, free CRM that offers contact management, email marketing, task automation, and more. With a user-friendly interface, it's suitable for LLCs of all sizes and integrates well with various business tools.

Salesforce: A leader in CRM software, Salesforce is a comprehensive tool offering various features, from sales pipeline management to marketing automation. Salesforce is highly customizable, allowing you to tailor it to your business needs.

Zoho CRM: Zoho offers a flexible, cost-effective CRM tool for small businesses and startups. It includes features like lead generation, contact management, email marketing, and analytics to help improve sales processes and customer relationships.

4. Marketing Tools and Resources

Effective marketing is essential to growing your LLC and attracting more customers. From managing social media to creating email campaigns, the right marketing tools can make a huge difference in your business's visibility.

Mailchimp: Mailchimp is one of the most popular email marketing platforms available. It allows you to create and send email campaigns, track their performance, and automate marketing workflows. Mailchimp also offers powerful segmentation tools to help you target the right audience.

Hootsuite: Social media management tools like Hootsuite are essential for keeping track of your brand's presence on multiple platforms. With Hootsuite, you can schedule posts, monitor engagement, and analyze performance across social networks.

Canva: Visual content is a key component of any marketing strategy. Canva is a user-friendly design tool that allows you to create stunning graphics, presentations, and social media posts without advanced design skills.

5. Legal Tools

As an LLC owner, ensuring that you stay compliant with legal requirements and protect your intellectual property is vital. Legal tools can help you draft contracts, manage trademarks, and stay on top of regulatory changes.

LegalZoom: LegalZoom provides affordable legal services for LLC owners. Whether you need help drafting contracts, filing patents or trademarks, or forming your LLC, LegalZoom offers various services tailored to entrepreneurs.

Rocket Lawyer: Rocket Lawyer provides online legal resources, including document creation tools, contract templates, and access to legal advice. Their services are a great option for small businesses looking to handle their legal needs quickly and cost-effectively.

6. Discounts and Deals on Popular Business Software

In addition to the essential tools listed above, many business software providers offer special discounts and deals for small businesses and LLC owners. Taking advantage of these discounts can help you reduce costs while still gaining access to powerful software. Below are some of the most popular business software providers that offer exclusive deals for LLC owners:

QuickBooks Discount for LLCs: Many business owners qualify for discounts when signing up for QuickBooks, which can help reduce costs on accounting software.

HubSpot Free and Discounted Plans: HubSpot offers free CRM and marketing tools, with the option to upgrade for more advanced features. Discounts are also available for LLC owners who sign up for multiple HubSpot services.

Canva for Nonprofits and Small Businesses: Canva offers discounted plans for nonprofit organizations and small businesses, which can be a huge cost-saving tool when creating marketing materials.

Access to the right tools and resources can make a world of difference for LLC owners looking to grow, manage, and streamline their businesses effectively. This **Exclusive Business Resource Toolkit** provides a curated selection of software, apps, and services to help you tackle essential tasks

like accounting, project management, customer relationship management, marketing, and legal compliance. By leveraging these tools, you can reduce operational costs, enhance productivity, and ultimately position your LLC for long-term success. Furthermore, with discounts on many of these popular business tools, you can ensure that your LLC has access to the best resources without breaking the bank.

4. BUSINESS CREDIT CARDS: MANAGING EXPENSES AND BUILDING CREDIT.

In today's business environment, controlling finances is one of the most important components of running a successful LLC. A business credit card is one of the most effective financial tools for financial stability, flexibility, and growth. Whether you own a tiny business or manage a booming LLC, a business credit card helps you to separate your personal and business money, develop business credit, and receive incentives that may be reinvested in your firm.

A company credit card is more than simply a tool for making purchases; it helps manage cash flow, increase corporate liquidity, and provide access to financing when needed. It also protects your personal assets by keeping corporate

transactions apart from personal ones. With the appropriate attitude, using a company credit card may be an important element of your overall financial strategy. This tutorial will educate you on selecting the correct card, applying for it, and utilizing it effectively to secure your LLC's economic success.

Why a Business Credit Card is Important for LLC Owners

The decision to utilize a company credit card should be taken seriously. It has several major benefits that can help your LLC in the short and long run. Here are some of the main reasons why having a company credit card is important for LLC owners:

1. Separate personal and business finances.

One of the first things financial experts advise business owners to do is keep their personal and business finances separate. A business credit card allows you to accomplish exactly that. Mixing personal and corporate transactions can cause confusion during tax season and complicate bookkeeping. It also puts your personal assets in danger because using the same credit card for everything makes it easy to mix personal and corporate finances.

A specialized business credit card allows you to keep your personal and professional costs separate. This division will give you a clean and orderly financial record, making it easier to track business spending, submit taxes, and manage cash flow. It also makes it easier to prove your LLC's spending if required for audits.

2. Improving Business Credit

Like individuals, businesses must establish credit to gain access to better financing choices, attractive loan conditions, and cheaper interest rates. A company credit card is one of the most effective ways to develop and grow your LLC's credit profile.

Company credit is distinct from personal credit, and a strong company credit score can lead to increased credit limits, better lending opportunities, and more favorable supplier terms. Managing your company credit card responsibly — paying bills on time, keeping your balance low, and managing credit wisely — will help your LLC's creditworthiness over time.

3. Maximizing financial flexibility.

A company credit card provides great financial freedom to your LLC. It enables you to manage cash flow more effectively, especially during high expenses or low revenue. If you experience a brief shortfall or need to make a significant purchase, having a credit line, particularly for your business, will allow you to continue functioning without depleting your personal funds or falling into financial troubles.

Business credit cards frequently have high credit limits, which can be handy for covering huge purchases or funding unforeseen charges. It acts as a cushion, allowing you to keep day-to-day business operations running smoothly even if your revenue is unexpected.

4. Earn rewards and cashback.

Many company credit cards have enticing incentive programs that might help your LLC. These incentives may include rebates, travel points, or discounts on certain company services. For example, you could get cash back on office supplies, marketing charges, or travel expenses. These awards can be reinvested in the firm, allowing you to save money on future purchases or even lower operational costs.

Maximizing rewards entails selecting the best business credit card for your needs and spending habits. For example, if your company routinely purchases office supplies or advertising, a card that offers generous rewards in these areas may be advantageous. Understanding how the rewards program works will enable you to make intelligent spending decisions that benefit your LLC long-term.

5. Streamlining expense tracking and management.

Business credit cards offer a structured approach to managing expenses and tracking business spending. All transactions are immediately tracked and categorized when you use a company credit card. Many credit cards also provide online tools and apps for monitoring expenditures, tracking expenses, and generating reports.

This can save time on bookkeeping, making it easier to create financial statements, manage profits, and preserve accurate records for tax purposes. Monthly company credit card statements allow you to easily evaluate and categorize costs, reducing errors and enhancing overall financial management.

How to Select the Right Business Credit Card for Your LLC

Choosing the best business credit card for your LLC depends on your company's unique needs, goals, and spending habits. While all company credit cards have similar features, such as credit limits and incentive programs, the optimal card for your LLC will depend on how you want to use it.

Here are some important considerations to consider when selecting a business credit card:

1. Reward Structure

Look for a card that rewards your LLC's most frequent spending areas. For example, if you travel regularly for business, you may want to consider a card that provides rewards or returns on travel expenses. Similarly, if your company spends a lot on office supplies, a card with more rewards for office supplies may be more useful. Compare rewards programs to see which one best meets your company's expenses.

2. Interest Rates & Fees

Business credit cards may have different interest rates and charge structures. Some credit cards provide 0% APR on purchases for an initial period, which might benefit new LLCs that need to spread payments out over time. However, ensure you are informed of the continued interest rates once the promotional period is over.

Be sure to include annual fees, transaction costs, and foreign transaction fees. Look for a card that adds value through rewards and advantages while reducing fees that could cut into your profits.

3. Credit Limit

Business credit cards normally have higher credit limits than personal credit cards, but the exact amount depends on your creditworthiness, business income, and financial history. A bigger credit limit allows for more flexibility when making significant purchases, which may be advantageous as your firm grows.

4. Additional perks and benefits.

Business credit cards include extra benefits like travel insurance, longer product warranties, and free access to financial management tools. These perks, in addition to the awards, can help improve the operations of your LLC and provide value to your firm.

How To Apply for A Business Credit Card.

Applying for a company credit card is a fairly straightforward process. Below is a step-by-step approach to applying for a business credit card:

1. Check your credit score.

Before applying for a company credit card, you should verify your personal and corporate credit scores. Many business credit cards, particularly ones with generous incentives and low interest rates, demand a strong credit history. If your credit score is worse than expected, you should consider raising it before applying.

2. Gather necessary information.

When applying for a business credit card, you must supply certain information, such as your LLC's legal name, address, tax identification number (EIN), annual revenue, and expected business expenses. You may also be asked to submit information on the business founders' personal finances, particularly if your company is young and has no credit history.

3. Compare card offers.

Review various business credit card offers to locate the one that best fits your needs. Attention to interest rates, incentive programs, fees, and other card-related benefits. Once you decide on the best option, you may complete the application online or with a representative.

4. Submit the application.

Once you've completed the application, submit it for approval. The credit card issuer will review your financial history and business information to assess eligibility. If authorized, you will receive your new business credit card by mail.

Maximizing Financial Flexibility

Using a company credit card correctly can greatly increase your LLC's financial flexibility. It enables you to segregate your personal and corporate funds, establish business credit, and manage your LLC's spending while optimizing incentives and savings. Selecting the proper card and using it responsibly can lay a solid foundation for your company's financial health and success.

CONCLUSION

Navigating the Future of Your LLC

Creating and administering an LLC is a significant undertaking. As we have seen throughout this tutorial, founding, operating, and expanding a Limited Liability Company needs careful analysis, strategic planning, and continual diligence. However, while the steps may appear daunting, the benefits of forming a well-structured LLC that offers financial protection, operational flexibility, and long-term viability are significant. Understanding the foundations of LLC formation, taxation, legal requirements, and growth plans gives you the knowledge you need to guarantee that your firm flourishes in an ever-changing environment.

As you continue your LLC journey, remember that each stage of your company's lifecycle—from initial formation to scaling and expanding—requires ongoing learning and adaptability. The business world is constantly changing, with legislative changes, economic volatility, and technological improvements influencing how you interact with your market. Staying informed and nimble will allow you to manage these changes with confidence.

CREATING A SOLID FOUNDATION FOR LONG-TERM SUCCESS

The first stage in any company enterprise is to create a solid foundation. Forming an LLC and knowing the protections and benefits it provides is a critical component of this. By selecting the appropriate legal form for your company, you protect your personal assets while also obtaining flexibility in managing operations and taxes. Furthermore, understanding and adhering to state and federal requirements, obtaining enough insurance coverage, and establishing good financial management techniques are all critical components of your LLC's success.

Choosing the right insurance coverage, creating a comprehensive business marketing strategy, and leveraging tools like business credit cards to manage expenses are all important steps toward financial health and stability. Insurance protects you from unforeseen events, marketing strategies help attract and retain customers, and credit cards allow you to manage your cash flow while building your business credit. These tools work together to create a strong system that enables you to reduce risk while increasing development potential.

STAYING COMPLIANT AND FUTURE-PROOFING YOUR BUSINESS

Compliance is more than a legal responsibility; it is a strategic asset enabling you to establish a long-term business. Understanding annual reporting requirements, remaining current with tax regulations, and keeping your LLC in good standing will help you avoid costly legal or financial concerns in the future. Furthermore, ensuring that your company has a sound operating agreement in place, constantly revising it to reflect any changes, and planning for the potential of dissolution or termination can assist in maintaining transparency and reducing disagreements.

However, your LLC's ability to thrive is not simply determined by present operational methods. To ensure long-term success, you must anticipate and be prepared for future changes. The business landscape is continuously changing, with new legislation, tax reforms, and technological improvements influencing businesses' operations. By keeping an eye on developing trends, adjusting to new tools and systems, and remaining adaptable to your company strategy, you can position your LLC to be competitive for years.

GROWTH, INNOVATION AND MARKET EXPANSION

Another important feature of having a successful LLC is the opportunity to grow. Scaling your firm demands a combination of strategic forethought, adequate resources, and the ability to manage expansion efficiently. Scaling your LLC needs careful strategy and execution, whether you want to add workers, enter new markets, or develop strategic collaborations.

Technological advancements, particularly in the digital arena, are becoming increasingly important in all corporate strategies. Using digital marketing, e-commerce, and business management solutions will help you attract new customers, streamline processes, and increase your global reach. Furthermore, by adopting technology innovations, you position your company to compete with industry leaders while providing a better experience for your clients.

While expansion is necessary, it is as crucial to preserve your

LLC's principles and objectives as it grows. Maintaining the quality of your products or services, assuring client satisfaction, and developing a strong brand identity will assist your company in retaining customer loyalty and remaining competitive in an increasingly congested economy.

ADDRESSING CHALLENGES AND SEIZING OPPORTUNITIES

While the route to economic success is full of opportunity, it is also fraught with difficulties. As you establish and expand your LLC, you may encounter challenges such as shifting market conditions, new competitors, or changing client demands. The key to overcoming these problems is flexibility and resilience. Continuously reevaluating your ideas, soliciting customer input, and remaining adaptable can help you stay ahead of the curve.

One of the most important things you can do as an LLC owner is to be open to new ideas. The business world is continuously changing, and those who accept new ideas, technologies, and company models are likelier to succeed. Keep an eye on market trends, invest in R&D, and look for ways to partner with other businesses or thought leaders in your area.

Fostering an innovative and continuous improvement culture positions your LLC for long-term success.

Final Thoughts

Creating and operating an LLC is both a fun and demanding endeavor. As an LLC owner, you take on numerous roles, including entrepreneur, manager, strategist, and, occasionally, accountant. However, with the correct tools, resources, and mindset, you can negotiate the difficulties of business ownership and transform your LLC into a viable and long-term organization.

Remember that while the administrative chores associated with founding and administering your LLC may appear intimidating, they are critical for the preservation and success of your firm. By focusing on compliance, financial management, marketing, and growth plans, you may position yourself for success in a competitive and fast-paced business world.

Above all, remember how important it is to be adaptable and knowledgeable. The corporate environment is continuously evolving, and those who can adapt and pivot as needed are the ones who succeed. Take what you've learned from this guide and put it into action — create your LLC with purpose, secure it with strong legal and financial procedures, and scale it with creativity and innovation.

Finally, founding and expanding your LLC is a process that involves serious consideration, hard work, and strategic decision-making. Your LLC may grow into a robust, long-lasting firm with the correct mindset, tools, and resources.

KEY TERMS:

1. Limited Liability Companies (LLC)

An LLC is a business form that combines a corporation's limited liability with a partnership's tax flexibility. It shields the owners' personal assets from corporate liabilities, making it a popular choice among entrepreneurs.

2. Limited Liability Protection

This legal theory distinguishes between business owners' personal assets and the business's liabilities and debts. If the LLC is sued or has financial problems, the owner's personal assets (such as their homes and bank accounts) are usually safeguarded.

3. Operating Agreement.

An operating agreement is a legal document that describes the internal operations of an LLC. It covers the ownership structure, management, and financial arrangements. Although it is not usually required by state law, it is strongly advised because it helps to reduce disagreements among members.

4. Articles of Organization.

This is the official document filed with the state to establish an LLC. It usually contains the LLC's name, company address, and the names of its members. Once filed and authorized, the LLC is officially established.

5. Registered Agent.

A registered agent is a person or corporate entity authorized to receive legal documents on behalf of the LLC, such as lawsuits or government notices. The agent's physical address must be where the LLC is formed.

6. Pass-through Taxation

Pass-through taxation relates to how LLCs are taxed. Instead of the company paying taxes on its earnings, profits and losses are passed on to members, who record them on their personal tax returns. This avoids "double taxation" for corporations.

7. Self-employment Taxes

Self-employment taxes are paid by persons who work for themselves, including Social Security and Medicare. LLC members involved in the business are usually subject to self-employment taxes on their portion of the LLC's profits.

8. S-Corporation (S-Corp) Election

An S-Corp is a tax status that LLCs can choose to have. An LLC with this status can avoid self-employment taxes on a portion of its profits by designating owners as employees and paying them a reasonable remuneration. Any residual profits may be given as dividends.

9. C Corporation (C Corp)

A C-corporation is a corporate form in which the firm is taxed independently from its owners. LLCs can be taxed as C-Corps, but this may result in double taxation—once at the corporate level and then at the individual level when profits are distributed.

10. Business Credit.

Business credit refers to a company's capacity to borrow money or purchase goods and services on credit. Establishing company credit is critical for increasing financial reputation, distinguishing between personal and business funds, and obtaining future loans or credit lines.

11. Business Credit Cards

A business credit card that can be used for business purposes is issued to a company (rather than a person). It promotes financial separation between personal and business funds, boosts business credit, and provides various incentives such as cashback or points.

12. Financial Separation.

This refers to separating personal and business funds, which is critical for LLC owners. It guarantees that business expenses are properly defined, simplifying tax reporting and protecting personal assets in case of a lawsuit or business difficulties.

13. Business Insurance

Business insurance protects a company from financial loss caused by unanticipated events like accidents, property damage, or lawsuits. General liability, professional liability, and workers' compensation insurance are three common types of business insurance.

14. General Liability Insurance.

This is a basic sort of business insurance that covers claims for bodily injury, property damage, and personal injury. It is critical for addressing general hazards connected with running a firm.

15. Professional Liability Insurance.

Errors and omissions (E&O) insurance protects professionals from claims alleging negligence, mistakes, or failure to perform tasks.

16. Worker Compensation Insurance

Most states require firms with employees to get this sort of insurance. It covers medical expenses and missed pay for workers who are injured on the job.

17. Marketing Strategy.

A marketing strategy is a plan for contacting potential customers and promoting items or services. It entails identifying target markets, developing brand messages, and choosing promotional channels, including digital marketing, social media, and traditional media.

18. Digital Marketing.

Digital marketing is marketing activities that employ the internet or electronic devices. This can involve search engine optimization (SEO), email marketing, social media marketing, content marketing, and paid advertising on platforms like Google Ads.

19. Social Media Marketing.

Social media marketing entails leveraging networks such as Facebook, Instagram, LinkedIn, and Twitter to promote your company, interact with customers, and raise brand awareness. It's a crucial tool for businesses trying to reach a larger audience and communicate with their customers in real-time.

20. Brand Building

The brand building creates a distinct identity for your company that appeals to customers. It entails identifying your company's vision, values, and aesthetics and communicating them through communications, design, and customer experience.

21. Cash Flow Management.

Cash flow management entails monitoring and managing the flow of funds into and out of a business. Positive cash flow is required to sustain operations, pay personnel, purchase inventory, and invest in growth.

22. Profit margin.

The profit margin is the portion of income that exceeds the cost of production or operation. It is an important indicator for determining a business's profitability. Higher profit margins typically reflect more efficient operations.

23. Project Management Tools

Project management software enables firms to track and manage assignments, deadlines, and team participation. Asana, Trello, and Monday.com are popular project management software that helps teams stay on schedule and increase productivity.

24. Business Resource Toolkit.

A business resource toolkit is a curated collection of tools, software, and services intended to assist firms to streamline operations. Examples of such offerings include accounting software, marketing tools, project management platforms, and even business-related product discounts.

25. Joint ventures

A joint venture is a corporate structure in which two or more parties agree to pool resources for a specific project or business aim, sharing both rewards and risks. Joint ventures can help LLCs enter new markets and increase their capabilities.

26. Annual reports and fees.

Many states require LLCs to produce annual or biennial reports to keep their status. These reports often feature business-related information, such as changes in management or firm address, and there may be associated expenses.

27. State-Specific Compliance Requirements

LLCs must follow the laws and regulations of the state where they are registered. This includes filing annual reports, paying yearly fees, keeping a registered agent, and ensuring that the LLC's operating agreement and tax filings are correct.

28. Dissolution of an LLC.

Dissolution is the formal process of closing a business. When an LLC is dissolved, it indicates the company is no longer legally recognized and has been terminated. To dissolve an LLC officially, particular measures must be taken, such as settling debts and completing the relevant documents with the state.

29. Tax Deductions

Tax deductions enable businesses to decrease their taxable revenue by deducting specific expenses. Common LLC deductions include business costs, home office deductions, vehicle-related expenses, etc.

30. Self-employment Tax

The term "self-employment tax" refers to the tax placed on business owners who work for themselves, which includes Social Security and Medicare. This tax applies to LLC members who actively participate in the business and receive earnings.

31. Operating expenses.

Operating expenses are the costs of running a firm, such as rent, utilities, payroll, and other ongoing expenses. Keeping track of these expenses is critical to maintaining profitability.

These concepts form a good foundation for understanding an LLC's structure, management, and functioning. Each term ensures your LLC is legally compliant, financially healthy and ready for development.

www.ingramcontent.com/pod-product-compliance
Lightning Source LLC
Chambersburg PA
CBHW052200220526
45471CB00004B/1757